USED BOOK SALES

Less Work & Better Profits

DATE DUE

by R. Keith Crotz

Highsmith Press Handbook Series

Highsmith
P R E S S

Fort Atkinson, Wisconsin

This book would not have been possible without the understanding of Mary Ann, Will and Genny.

Published by Highsmith Press
W5527 Highway 106
P.O. Box 800
Fort Atkinson, Wisconsin 53538-0800
1-800-558-2110

© D. Keith Crotz, 1995
Cover art: Mary Ann Highsmith

The paper used in this publication meets the minimum requirements of American National Standard for Information Science — Permanence of Paper for Printed Library Material. ANSI/NISO Z39.48-1992.

Library of Congress Cataloging in Publication
    Crotz, D. Keith (Darrell Keith), 1954–
        Used book sales: less work & better profits / by
    D. Keith Crotz.
          p.   cm. -- (Highsmith Press Handbook series)
        Includes bibliographical references and index.
        ISBN 0-917846-32-X
        1. Antiquarian booksellers--United States. 2. Fund
    raising--United States. I. Title. II. Series.
Z479.C77 1995
381' .45002'0973--dc20   94-24316

Contents

Introduction

As continually shrinking budgets are stretched to pay for the ever-growing number of new books, technologies and services, the need to exploring improved fund-raising techniques is inevitable. Many organizations have made efforts in the past to "cash in" on the growing popularity of collectibles, either through displays, sales of unique association items, or auctions of donated articles. Although this is an option worth consideration, collectibles are of interest to a limited audience. Bake sales are nice, but non-sustaining. Book sales, however, appeal to a broad cross-section of the public. Very few people can boast that they have never read a book, or don't have at least a few books that rank as their favorites.

This informal guide will give you many of the strategies and tools needed to make money with books. Granted, it will take some time to organize, learn, sort, categorize, price and conduct a sale of used and donated books, but there are other benefits and cost savings that you already have working for you. Consider that the books are usually gifts. And if you are using volunteers, your only labor cost will be in guidance and training. Moreover, the books will benefit other readers by being recycled back into use through the sale.

While this book is directed towards libraries and other groups that sponsor book sales, it can be adapted on any scale for any organization, big or small, that wants to hold an "event" and have some cash left over when the dust settles. There is no better way to show support for your library or organization than to hand them a check large enough to buy needed equipment or new books. Best of all, you can have some fun in running a successful sale!

1
Book Sales at Their Worst and Best

Friends of the many libraries, university associations, clubs, churches, hospitals, chambers of commerce, service organizations, museums and retirement communities all hold book sales in one form or another. Some are well organized, others are fun to talk about, and others you'll never mention again and try to forget.

I can remember the very first book sale I ever attended that was conducted by a not-for-profit organization. As a professional bookseller, specializing in the narrowly focused field of agriculture and horticulture, I knew that there ought not to be all that many books to view, nor other folks interested in those books. *Wrong.*

My friend Dennis and I arrived about one hour early, and we were late. There must have been 50 people in front of us for this "white elephant" sale. We passed the time identifying other booksellers and discussing who would be after what books, then as the sale doors opened, folks who had never moved faster than a snail were off and running at a pace designed to exhaust an Olympic sprinter. Elbows flew, cutting people off as they rounded tables in pursuit of the perfect book. Library bags were strategically placed to trip those arriving second to a

table. It was chaos. The noise was deafening, as teams gleefully shouted their discoveries to one another.

At least the tables were organized by subject matter, which made book hunting a little easier. However, the room was too small for the number of tables, the aisles were too narrow, and there were unopened boxes of books under all of the tables. There's nothing more intoxicating to a bookseller at a sale than the books in unopened boxes *under* a table.

To top it all off, just as the adrenaline began to wear down, those of us lining up to pay discovered that there was one person at the cash box, totaling up the stacks, boxes, bags, and armloads of books. It was going to take longer to check out than it did to find the books.

I love talking with people. I love history and the development of modern technology as viewed from those present at the creation. I do not love having a well-meaning volunteer sitting behind a cigar-box, trying to make change for a $50 bill on a three dollar purchase with only $40 in change at the beginning of a sale.

I think you can see some of the real problems associated with holding a book sale of this type. Luckily, all of the hard-cover books were the same price, with a single, lower price for paperbacks. It is a large undertaking to price books individually and then to calculate all the prices at checkout time.

Fortunately, this sale was held on a single level store. Parking wasn't great, but it was adequate. Entry was in one door and out another. There was no fee to enter, and no other business was obstructed by the gathering crowds of attendees. Folks had to bring their own bags and boxes for their purchases. When that occurs, boxes can be a problem, for it reduces the space available on entering and some folks might trip over them. Whenever practical, keep a supply of empty boxes under the tables for customers to use. Restock each hour from another source other than full boxes under the tables. The errors I've described are just a few of the problems that can occur in a book sale. With good planning, they can be avoided.

I'm confident that each of you can close your eyes and remember a book sale that you either sponsored, participated in, or attended that contained many of the elements I've mentioned. By planning ahead you can avoid these problems at the next book sale in which you're involved.

On a grander scale

You can aim really high and emulate a southwestern friends of the library. They recently celebrated their 25th consecutive annual book sale. This three-day event attracts more than 20,000 people, requires 340 time slots and jobs for volunteers, and is staffed by nearly 200 people. Sally, who was the chairperson of the event, told me that she took off her pedometer when it reached the 100 mile mark on Saturday.

Twenty-eight volunteers pledge a minimum of four hours each week sorting and pricing the books as they come in. They work from many of the references you will read about in this volume. The boxes that they sort in

are donated by International Paper, and because the sale has grown too large for the library, the field house of the local university is offered at a modest fee. The facility has space for 18,000 cars, so parking is not a problem. Volunteers work throughout year boxing and organizing so that the 81 tons of books in 3,200 boxes can be transported from the library by Mayflower Van Lines. It takes only a few days to set-up the one million books around the field house.

Since this year's sale was the 25th anniversary of the friends group, anyone 25 years old was admitted free to the Friday night preview. All others, members included, had to pay the four dollar admission. It was a great marketing strategy.

The book sale is free on Saturday, and on Sunday the fun begins. All books are one dollar per shopping bag at the opening, and between 2:00 p.m. and 4:00 p.m. on Sunday, all books are free! All that remained of the one million books stocked at the beginning of the sale was 2,500 books.

Often the remaining books are donated during the sale to Veteran's Administration hospitals, community hospitals, schools and even the county jail and state prison. As you work with these groups, you will learn what kinds of books and magazines they can use and will take. This is a perfect way for those who have a sale, and don't want to deal with the left-overs, to put them to good use.

Advertising for the sale is done through the libraries, on local radio where some wonderful work is donated for prime time, and in a few select trade journals and local publications. The sale grossed over $55,000 this year. It's a wonderful example to emulate. Sally told me that the most important aspect of the sale is pricing the books so that people know that they are fair. Her selections of the better books draws booksellers and collectors from around the country. "Use price guides judiciously," she cautioned. "They reflect buying trends in different parts of the country." I'm already looking forward to attending the sale next year!

2

How This Book Will Help Your Sale

Having spent fifteen years involved in the bookselling trade, I've examined the pros and cons of sales with great interest. I even reached a point of specialization where I no longer attended sales, but rather was called in to evaluate books and assist in pricing them for the sponsoring organization. Flea markets, church bazaars and even garage sales helped me learn about good books, better books, collectible books and even rare books. In most general areas of books, I know enough to be dangerous. After all, a little learning is a dangerous thing. In other areas, such as children's books and cookbooks, I maintain a policy of benign neglect. After five years in the book business, I had a number of scouts attending the sales for me. These scouts were armed with lists of books wanted by my customers.

These book scouts are one of the important clients that libraries and other book sale sponsors will encounter. They may possess lists of books wanted for as many as ten booksellers across the country in as many specialties. Book scouts are an important link in making your book sale successful. Booksellers themselves may be one of the most essential elements in the success of a sale. You may find that one local used, rare and out-of-print bookshop that will pay more for five books donated for the sale than the rest of the thousands of lesser priced items. Making sure you find and correctly mark those five books is going to be very important to your sale.

After reading what follows, your organization will be able to mobilize volunteers to move, sort, categorize, grade, price, display, advertise, market, sell, and package large quantities of used cloth and paperback books for booksellers around the country. You'll learn how to organize sale tables so that similar subject categories are nearby, and how to keep from mixing poetry with the hunting and fishing books, as well as how to clear tables of their books at the end of a sale.

Why donate your time for 50¢ per book when those very books are worth five or ten dollars or more to the right person. Learn to find those customers and then all you have to do is let those prospective customers know about your sale.

Learn to recognize the winners and losers. There are more valuable titles out there than *Reader's Digest* condensed books. I would not even accept them for your sale. Politely suggest that they be used to balance the Christmas tree stand.

You'll learn the buzz words of the book business. What differentiates an endpaper from a fly-leaf, a first edition from a reprint. There is a world of authors in many fields that aren't found in the pages of the *New York Times* best seller list, or in other popular press reviews. Who are they? Do you recognize Jerome Charyn? Would you like to own the Naval Institute edition of Mr. Clancy's *Hunt For Red October*? Who buys what type of book? How many different subject areas are there for collectible books? Wouldn't it be easier to send a 19¢ post card and sell a book for a hundred dollars than to watch people mishandle it on a table marked at ten dollars, wishing you knew someone who would actually offer you a fair price for it? How will you know what a fair price for an individual book is? Can a paperback be worth more than a cloth bound book? What are the factors that make a book valuable?

Each chapter will build your knowledge of books, with resources for supplemental reading in the bibliographies at the end of this book. I've even included an appendix about simple repair so titles in marginal condition can be offered for more money. I have also suggested several ways you can promote the sale with the most publicity for the least amount of capital outlay.

If you put as many of the tips and techniques as possible into practice, your organization's efforts will be rewarded. Your volunteers will feel they have been part of a positive experience. They'll be taking home new, treasured friends from your sale. Area merchants may experience increased business from the out-of-town customers your event draws, and the good news that reaches the community will encourage future donations. Consider the impact of the headline, "Friends of the Library donates $5,000." Your volunteer base might grow as a result of such a successful sale.

3

Volunteers

The most important factor for a successful book sale is a strong volunteer base or friends group. The book sale workforce need not be large, but it must be dedicated. The group need not be a formal organization…just eager to learn and work. To make sure your sale is a success, however, it helps if there are rules and expectations in advance. Putting together the volunteer work force may take a whole year's advance planning. (There are several references on recruiting and developing volunteers in the appendix IV.)

Recruitment

Advertising for interested volunteers should not be too conspicuous or you'll tip your hand too early as to what you're planning, and others will borrow your fund-raising idea. Signs placed in the library or at your organization's principle meeting place should serve as a good drawing card for interested participants. An organizational meeting is critical. You will need to recruit a chairperson or chief, if only to interface with the officials of the organization for whom the proceeds are destined. This individual has to have sufficient leadership skills and organizational abilities to keep

the workers focused. It would not be asking too much for interested candidates to fill out a form listing their strengths, prior experience, interests in the world of books, and available hours. In this day and age, the competition for competent volunteers is incredible.

Organizing your book sale in the most professional manner possible is one primary means to attract the good volunteers. Be certain that the volunteers are differentiated from others associated with the library or organization. A free tee-shirt or other recognizable badge goes a long way toward establishing an identity. A good library supply catalog will contain a number of items at reasonable cost.

When reviewing the interests of your volunteer candidates, keep in mind their physical condition. Will they be able to handle 30 boxes of fiction at 60 pounds per box? Have a representative sample of the books recommended in appendix I (A Bibliography on Book Collecting) available for their review to identify interests. Be certain that the volunteer leaders discuss and develop reasonable work schedules. Without a work schedule and the necessary tools, the chairperson and other officers will find themselves burning the midnight oil in an effort to finish the sorting and pricing, or the other key elements of the sale. Keep track of the volunteer hours expended on the project. In some instances, it counts towards community grants and awards. Initially, the chairperson should make him or herself available whenever possible to keep the educational curve moving upward, and to encourage the troops as they discover just how much work they will have.

Job assignments

With an established friends group, one of the problems I have seen develop is that several people want the same job. I can't solve your problem, but I can stress that division of labor must be observed. All relevant subject areas must be covered with as little overlap as possible. The workers must feel as if the subject areas they are responsible for are theirs! With a friends organization, try to involve those who have not been overly aggressive in their commitment to the group. Stress how essential the tasks are, and the personal satisfaction they will receive on seeing the neatly sorted tables of books on sale day. I would also offer one word of caution for volunteers and friends. Those who sort the books, price the books, and arrange the books for the sale, should be an assigned group. You'll be amazed how many eager participants you'll have on set-up day, anxious to drop a gem or two of a title into a waiting bag as they move sorted and priced books from the boxes onto the tables.

Having covered the people-power background for a book sale, now is as good a time as any to outline some of the duties of your volunteer army. The most difficult task in any book sale is storage and sorting capacity. You need an area large enough to store the donated books easily, room to move the sorted and boxed books and easy access to your place of sale. While it may seem like double duty in sorting and storing the books for the sale prior to pricing, this

double handling affords you the opportunity to classify and select the best books. These are the books that will provide you with the best return, while you can keep the run-of-the-mill titles sorted together by subject. When your sorting is nearly done, you can begin to price the better books. All the while your crews have been sorting, they should also be reading from the selected literature in appendix I to this volume.

One of the questions that should be asked on the volunteer application is "What books interest you?" Now's the time to put that information to work. You'll need to develop specialists for sorting in areas such as homes and gardens, home repair, religion, fiction, children's literature, cookbooks, business, computers, magic, art, mystery, science fiction and other areas that appear in the mountain of boxes that need to be sorted. It is important to keep the same people working in their subject area. Sorting parties should be held once a month or as needed on a regular basis in order to keep the work-flow smooth.

Organization

Here's what should happen in preparing for a successful sale. The library or organization receives books as donations. Unless otherwise specified, these books are the property of the recipient and can be dealt with as seen fit, that is, they are either added to the collection or *sold*. The donations are boxed or otherwise housed in the work area. Sorting is best done on tables, in order to avoid the constant strain of bending. At a short distance behind the sorting tables are tables with signs marking the categories outlined above. As the donated books are examined, they are placed in their corresponding places on the back tables. Hurt, damaged or inappropriate items are easy to remove at this time. A short training session showing examples of each category is highly recommended.

It is a good idea to have an active box solic-
itation program associated with the organization of your event. Accept only sturdy
boxes, in good condition. Book boxes from
moving companies are the best because of
their standard size. You might even consider asking local companies such as U-
Haul, Ryder or a professional moving company for donations. Point out the publicity
you are prepared to offer them!

It does not take a large workforce to sort the
books, as long as your organization keeps
them sorted on a regular basis. Posting
signs in the library advertising for donations is a good way to start solicitating for
help. As I've mentioned before, you'll not
want to advertise for donations too soon,
for fear of tipping your hand to another
organization. *But*, be sure to specify a time
frame. It is very difficult to cope with donations received the afternoon before the sale.
Set those donations aside and worry about
them next year.

Your specialists do not need to begin their
work on further sorting and pricing until
there are several full boxes in each category. We'll turn to the steps in setting-up
the sale in the next chapter. Pricing is one
of the most important steps in generating
better profits through your book sale, and
we'll cover that in chapter 5.

4

Sale Set-Up

Once you have the books sorted, culled and ready to price, your chairperson can begin to get a feel for the number of subjects selected. Checking with your librarian regarding the subjects of books most often circulated from the building will provide a good idea of popular categories in your area.

While we've not yet discussed pricing books, now is a good time to outline how to prepare for the sale. All of the advice I'm about to impart revolves around the best case scenario, that is, if you were to build a facility solely for conducting used book sales, here is what you'd have.

Site selection

Avoid a location that requires books to be moved up or down stairs. Books are very heavy and require herculean efforts to move them. If you have stairs, you'll know what I mean as your donations accumulate. You'll want to sort, store, price and prepare the sale as close to one location as possible. The event need not necessarily be held at the library or your organization's venue, but try not to have to pay rental fees and other costs in moving the book sale to the "ideal" location. If you do not have the perfect

location, see what can be arranged with a local school or arena for the use of their facility for the sale. Try not to pay any rent if possible. Offer them two percent of the net sales if they require compensation. Note that your organization is working to better your community and stress how they are involved in advancing the quality of town life.

Whenever possible, use a standard book box for storing and handling books. They can hold a maximum of 60 pounds of books, fit through doorways with ease and stack easily. Bigger boxes only exhaust the volunteers. All of the boxes of sorted books should be clearly marked on the outside flaps, as to the categories inside. All the boxes of one category must be stored together to ease the assembly of the sale. If possible enlist the aid of a local service group such as the Girl Scouts, Boy Scouts, 4-H or Kiwanis Key Club should you have to move the books in order to hold the sale.

Subject categories

I would recommend an in-depth look at categories you might want to consider. For an exhaustive look at categories, I suggest *Antiquarian, Specialty, and Used Book*

Sellers, edited by James and Karen Ethridge. Their publication lists 134 pages of subjects or categories used by professional booksellers.

The most common categories are those associated with leisure activities: gardening, cookbooks, sports, woodworking, sewing and related crafts, genealogy, art, literature, fiction, mysteries, detective fiction (we're splitting hairs now). Other categories that are popular are horror, science fiction, and fantasy. It would take another small volume to explain the differences between the last three. I would also suggest the history of individual states, music, religion, books about books, body building, book collecting, circus, Civil War, World War I and II, children's books, and fishing. I think you're beginning to get the picture. Some of the above categories will only become evident as you sort the books. You'll probably even invent some categories of your own.

Of course you'll have to sort some of the categories, such as fiction, mysteries, horror, science fiction, and crime by binding type. There's cloth, (or hard-cover) and paperback. You need not even keep the same categories sorted by cover type together. Often in sales, it pays to keep the paperbacks separate from the hard-cover books, especially in the realm of literature. There are those who are out to complete their collection of a particular author and they know exactly what they are after, while other book sale attendees are readers, only interested in finding an affordable and portable copy of an author's work. The former wants first editions, in their original dust jacket, while the later wants any paperback copy that's complete and unabridged. Keeping the cloth hard-covers of narrative works on one side of the room and the paperbacks of that same group on another will assure brisk sales.

The paperback and cloth hard-covers of most other categories may be sorted and boxed together. Buyers will often be interested first with the non-fiction or how-to books, while the type of binding will be of secondary importance, as long as the condition of the book isn't disintegrated.

One especially fortunate Chicago suburban library has overflow shelf space in an unused basement area. As the books for the sale are sorted, they are placed on shelves in designated areas, then local booksellers come through and check for any special value books. Then the books are taken down, priced and readied for the sale. That way the books only have to be handled two times prior to the sale, and placed into a box for movement only once.

Most facilities are not so fortunate to have available space and are forced to handle the books a number of times prior to the sale. I wish I had an answer for this. Unless you can arrange storage at the site of a sale, or you have sufficient room at the sale location, hauling book boxes is part of the price you pay for community involvement.

I have been to book sales in tents out-of-doors, larger than anything the Ringling Brothers had to offer. I've been to an arena in Wisconsin where there must have been 500,000 books. I routinely read in the *AB Bookman* about sales on the East Coast with even more books. Such sales may last for a week, twelve hours each day, and require many volunteers working several days every week for a whole year. A local college field house or other large facility, even a warehouse would not be out of the question.

Sale floor plan

Once you have chosen a site, arranged for the delivery of the books, planned the table locations, and assembled the volunteers, the books for the sale are normally placed on standard 8' x 28" tables. Make sure you have planned in advance for the right number of tables, estimated the needed space, and made a layout. Please refer to the sample diagram of a viable layout included in this text. (figure one) Each standard book

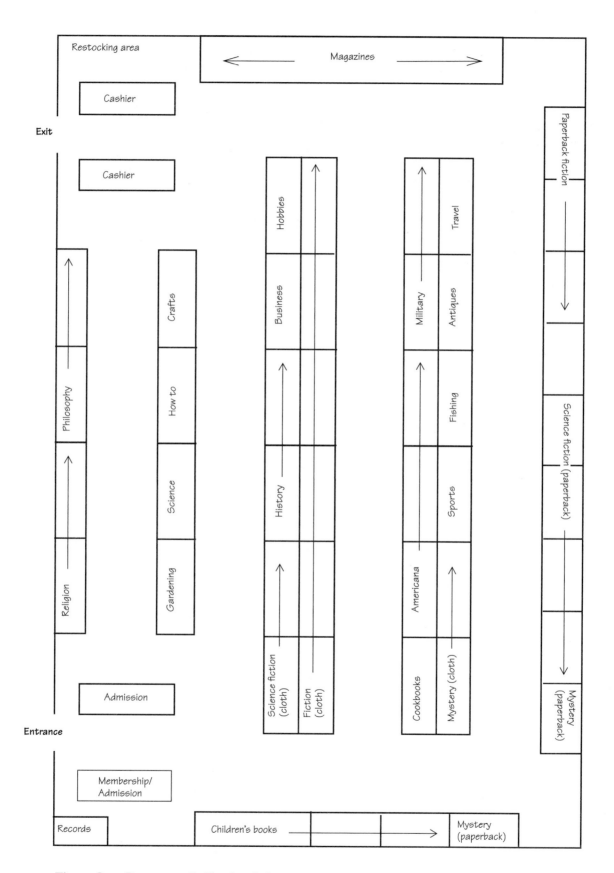

Figure One: Recommended book sale layout.

box of one and a half cubic feet holds about four linear feet of hard-cover books. The standard table should hold six boxes, arranged in three long rows.

Book display

To ease the hunt for the perfect book, customers generally prefer books arranged fore-edge down, with the spine showing. The rows of books should have their spines oriented in the same direction, so that customers can read the book titles on their side of the table. Tables should be arranged two wide with an aisle on either side. This prevents people from reaching across and grabbing a book out from under the nose of a person on the opposite side of a table. Remember, the folks at the sale are passionate bookpeople, and some of the finer social graces might be temporarily forgotten. Be sure to keep just one subject on a side. That will keep the distribution of customers in each aisle more uniform.

I have already cautioned about storing your books under the tables for restocking. People can't resist the temptation to look inside and help you stock the tables. Always keep at least a 4' space for an aisle between the tables. People will be filling boxes between their feet with carefully guarded books, and if there are books available for viewing from both sides of the table, 4' is the minimum distance for avoiding crowded aisles. If tables are placed against the walls, it is best to keep them only one table wide.

Paperbacks should fit five rows across, with up to eight or more boxes filling an 8' x 2' table. The books should always have all the titles oriented the same direction on a table for ease in scanning the titles by the customers. This will take some additional time during the initial setup, but it will result in better sales. Whenever possible, fill a table with just one category. Always use bookends to support the titles. I have seen some sale volunteers place a stack of books at the end of each row on a table. These stacks of books will be picked up and examined, allowing the long neat rows of titles an easy, quick and noisy fall to the floor. Most folks are not inclined to examine a bookend too closely. Have your volunteers constantly straightening the tables. It is very difficult to recover your straight rows once they disintegrate. The tables of books will need regular attention every fifteen minutes. Remember to restock your tables from a different location other than from boxes under the tables. Behind the scenes organization is just as important as what the public gets to see. During the sale some customers will quickly fill their boxes and bags from the tables, and then retire to a corner to sort through what they have gathered. As they make piles of unwanted books, have a volunteer take them back to a staging area for restocking at the end of the day's sale. The restocking area need not be large for the average sale, just enough room to make a few stacks on the floor or on a spare table or two. At the end of the day, the books can be returned to their correct table and subject classification or they can be boxed and allocated to organizations that are to receive books after the sale.

Signage

People always arrive early for the sale. Be sure that there are signs visible that show the layout of the tables. It will allow for less congestion during that first mad dash for the books.

While people are standing in line, have signs posted thanking all of the people, groups and businesses that made the event possible. Saying "thank you" to as many people as possible is one way of guaranteeing cooperation for future events.

Have your volunteers make several sturdy, well-lettered signs for each category. The signs should tower above the books by a good 3' and should be visible from both sides of the table. The signs should have letters large enough to be seen from approximately 20' away. A great way to promote the book sale is by publication of a map of the intended layout for the sale, showing the location of all the different categories. Make sure you indicate the exits and the location of the cashiers.

Here are some additional points to ponder when producing posters or other promotional information regarding the book sale. Indicate the location, days, times of the sale and any special instructions regarding parking and access to the sale. Pay special attention to any admission charge. It often does no harm to charge a one dollar fee, noting that the proceeds benefit a specific fund within the sponsoring organization. The entry fee is particularly feasible for small sales. Note if there will be a preview night, open only to members of the friends of the library or other sponsoring organization. The preview night is an excellent method of raising additional funds from the sale.

Building membership

Membership in your organization can grow as a result of the preview. For example, if membership in the Friends of the Library is five dollars and good for one year, you could allow members of your friends group to attend the sale for free. Non-members might be invited to attend for a six dollar preview fee. Be certain to have a table in front of the entrance to the sale where memberships may be purchased. Laud the other benefits available to members of your group, not just the advance admission!

Any professional book scouts, booksellers, and collectors are certain to join, not only to save the dollar, but to be notified in advance of the next sale. Your membership should receive notification of any sales or unusual donations throughout the year. If you are particularly well organized, your membership form will list areas of bookish interest, and your membership software will have a subject or category sort function so you can target a specific audience for future events. The professionals who attend the event will greatly appreciate receiving your mailings and you may cultivate some

professional relationships that will be very valuable in the future. More on that to follow.

Crowd control

Be sure to have the sale entrance and exit at two opposite, well-marked locations to alleviate any bottlenecks. One way to keep the crowd from pushing and shoving their way in, is to send several teams of volunteers down the rows of anxious people on preview night, requesting to see membership cards, collecting the admission fee if they are not members, selling memberships for those who know the value of a dollar, and stamping hands with some signifying inked object to identify those who can be admitted. This advance registration for those in line will simplify admission and assure an increase in your membership.

If you produced a map of the sale with each table marked as to the subject category it contains, the waiting previewers will be most appreciative to receive it as they anxiously stand in line. The table locations of the books they are seeking will help them better plan their selection.

Handling cash

Plan to have three or more cashiers working at any one time even for the smallest book sale events. People are going to have arm loads, boxes and bags full of books, and they will be pushing, shoving and dropping their books in shuffling processions to the checkout lines. Each cashier should have a helper who reads the prices for the cashier to write down or enter into a register if the sale is particularly large and well organized. The cashier can then quickly total the purchases, money can change hands, and the next customer can be served.

Cash is the best form of payment for such events, although I know that the larger sales will take checks and some are even equipped for credit card purchases. Be careful about taking checks from those you don't know. Recovery can be very difficult, time consuming and frustrating. Always get the phone number and a picture identification of any person using a check to pay for their purchases. I know it slows down the process, but it's a must.

While we're on the subject of cash, there are a few details that should be covered regarding the flow of cash. If your organization plans to sell books throughout the year, your board of trustees or governing body should determine whether a sales permit is needed. In addition, you must determine well in advance of the event whether sales tax must be collected on the sales of the books and related items. Your town or city clerk will have some knowledge. Often the best place to check is with the County Clerk. Visit them in person and explain the purpose of your book sale. Have copies of your federal IRS 501(c)(3) tax exemption documents available. Be aware of the fact that some states may still require your organization to collect sales taxes even though the federal government considers your organization to be charitable and/or educational.

Stimulating sales

The goal of the book sale is to sell as many of the books as possible. A three day event is the best, with a members' and paid admission preview on a Friday evening, a general admission of a dollar per person Saturday, and free admission on Sunday. The hours of the sale should not put too great a strain on your already tired volunteers. Friday night should run from 5:00 to 9:00 p.m., Saturday from 9:00 a.m. to 5:00 p.m., and Sunday from 12:00 to 4:00 p.m. These hours will give most members of the public an opportunity to attend the sale. On Sunday, all books should be half their marked price in order to further decrease the remaining stock, and the last hour should feature all boxes of books at two dollars. This bargain will attract those who would normally not have the patience to come back on the last day. At two dollars

per box, you will be assured of not having to contend with too many books to pack and return to your staging area.

Your primary goal at this point in time is to get rid of the remaining books. If a customer has a bagful of books, that's fine too. Just encourage them to take away as many books as possible. Books for free during the last hour or two of the sale is the best way to clear the tables and make the job of cleaning up after the sale easier.

A fun way to dispose of 25 or so of the best books is to hold an auction from 8:00 to 9:00 p.m. on the night of the preview. Set up chairs if space permits. If possible, print a handbill describing the books and why they are important. The printed handbill will allow you an opportunity to start the bidding at levels not otherwise possible. Remember that condition is important! If you can entice a local celebrity or sports figure into participating in the auction, the crowd appeal will be even better. Plan to serve refreshments for the auction, another method for making some additional funds during the sale.

One last word of advice on volunteers. Keep them happy! Maintain two volunteers in reserve at a modest sale to relieve others for a short break during the sale. Have hot and cold drinks available, light snacks and maybe even jelly doughnuts for those in the trenches. If your volunteers are well taken care of during the sale, then it will run without a glitch, and you'll enjoy a return of seasoned veterans for next year's sale.

Negotiating Prices

Everyone loves a bargain. At members-only or preview nights there should not be much room for negotiation of the price. Your prime goal is to make money for your organization, and it's just too early in the process to adjust the prices. There's every chance that another individual will gratefully purchase the book at the price marked. Explain the rationale to potential buyers and tell them that there will be special prices on the books as the book sale moves from day to day. Tell them they're welcome to wait and see if the book is still available then! That should be enough to entice them to buy.

Make sure that your volunteers are made aware of the policy, and be sure that it is enforced consistently. It is important that everyone know that they will be handled the same. Pushy individuals should not be allowed to intimidate your volunteers.

Don't allow a visiting bookseller to talk you down on an item the first day of the sale. Booksellers will impress you with their vast knowledge of a book or author, but be firm. If you have done your research carefully, there will be sufficient room for a bookseller's profit.

Price negotiation is possible prior to the close of the second day (of a three day event), and for a book or two, not an armful or boxful. When asked whether you'll accept a lower price for an item, take the book from the customer and examine it closely, as if lost in thought. If the offer is between 10 to 30% of the marked price, accept the offer. The discussion should be as quiet as possible, and then you should proceed with them to the cashier and inform your volunteer of the new price.

Handling leftovers

Working with booksellers in the area should solve your problems of what to do with the leftover books from the sale. Be sure to plan for the disposal of any unsold items well in advance of the sale. An ideal situation is to have one or more booksellers collect the books the morning after the sale and dispose of them. I am often called on to haul away unsold books from the sales at small town libraries within a 50 mile radius of my shop. I rarely find any books of much value, but it allows me a chance to keep my senses keen and handle a great many different kinds of books. I can funnel the books to the local museum for their book sale, which occurs in mid-January every year. I

take the time to sort through the boxes if I have to, but I normally prefer that the sponsoring library or organization leave the books on the tables. That allows me to do my own sorting as I review the tables. It is a perfect opportunity for me to find books for friends whose reading interests I know. We have a small paperback exchange in my town of 5,000 people and I always try and take the paperbacks there. The owner is most appreciative of the increased stock and all members of the surrounding community benefit. Of course, there are those books that I won't haul away. The sponsoring organization must toss them out. Books like law and accounting text books from 1933 just don't have much of a ready market. Whenever possible, these books should go to a recycling facility. Don't rely on just one bookseller, unless that's all you have. The local paperback exchanges should be eager for merchandise for the price of a single pickup!

Explain to the booksellers that this is a great chance for them to add to their inventory for only the cost of their time, and that many of the books may already be priced for them. Pick up of books from the huge tent and arena events is impossible for small booksellers, and these are often sold to the highest bidder as one large lot, or sent off to various hospitals, charities, nursing homes or the recycling facility. The small organization is not equipped to store books from sale to sale, and even as their sale is winding down, new donations are probably arriving for next year.

Donating a number of boxes of various subjects to hospitals, nursing homes, the county jail or your state's penitentiary are excellent ways to further benefit society as a whole from your sale. Goodwill, the Salvation Army, and other service organizations may have a use for your unsold donations. Contact them several weeks in advance of the sale to make the offer and formalize any details if necessary.

If you decide to hold some of the donated books over from one sale to the next, be certain that you have a facility for storage that is not too hot, not too cold and just right in terms of humidity. Books appreciate a temperature around 70 degrees Fahrenheit with a relative humidity of 50%. It will be impossible to attain the storage parameters at all times, but be aware of them. Keep the boxes of books off the floor and on wooden pallets whenever possible to improve airflow.

For long periods of time, books should be stored flat on their sides to prevent broken hinges or cocked bindings. Never store books more than four boxes high as it will put undue pressure on the spines, even in boxes.

A uniform box size is best. Whenever possible store the books in containers of similar size. It makes stacking easier, provides uniform protection for the books and makes handling and moving them more efficient. Contact the self-moving companies, the professional moving lines and perhaps a corrugated box manufacturer if you're in a metropolitan area, and request a donation.

♪
Pricing

Perhaps the most difficult part of organizing a book sale as a fund raising event is pricing the books. I have assisted several friends of the library groups to organize their book sales as books were received, sorted and boxed, then placed on the tables for the sale. Often, all hardback books were priced at 50¢ and paperbacks were a dime. That's the easy and painless way, but it short changes your organization by severely limiting your profits. It will make you most appreciated and somewhat ridiculed by the professional book community. If you place a signed first edition of Hemingway's *Three Stories & Ten Poems*, in paperback, dated 1923, on the fiction table at ten cents, you've just let a $6,000 book slip through your hands. You'd be better advised to contact a specialist bookseller of Hemingway books rather than offer it at your book sale. You'll learn about working with booksellers directly.

When I chaired the volunteer book sale at our local cultural institution, I was amazed to discover that a select group of individuals worked year-round checking out-of-print and in-print prices in published price guides, then putting half of the listed price on the front free endpaper of the book in pencil. While this can be time consuming, it

can assure you of an excellent return on your donated books. While it may also make collectors and book professionals grumble, you won't be giving the books away and the customers will still have room for bargains and happy discoveries.

One of the reasons for the meticulous sorting I've described is that it allows pricing to move along efficiently. By using volunteers who are most familiar with a given subject or category, they will have some exposure to prices, what's hot, what's not and which authors are popular. One of the best ways to prepare your book sale volunteers for pricing is to have them read a few of the selected titles in appendix III. These titles will provide the workers with a solid foundation in the philosophy of used book pricing as it applies to the everyday world of used and out-of-print books.

Condition

The single most important aspect of used book pricing is condition, condition, condition. Even a rare book from 1485 loses 75% of its value if the title page is lacking, pages are torn and missing and all of the illustrations are lacking. A modern book must be in a condition as similar as possible to how it was originally issued. See figure two for a sample page from a well-known price guide for an example of the description of different book conditions. If there was a dust jacket issued with the book, then it must be present for the book to match the values listed in the various price guides. People who collect books as a hobby or as an investment do not want notes and writing in their books, unless it's from a famous historical personality. Collectors want the books to be in original condition, without blemishes, damage or apologies. Unless the condition is right, the value of a book drops dramatically. The dust jacket alone can constitute 60% or more for the value of a modern first edition.

Your subject experts should work as needed to keep up with the flow of donations. Never allow the sorted boxes to get too far ahead of your pricing. With the books already sorted, their task will be easier and you'll achieve maximum value for your books. You'll not be able to find every title in every subject in a price guide or auction records. But after the first few boxes, a rhythm and feel for the books will develop. Have the pricers check the condition. They should check under the dust jacket when one is present to see that there aren't any hidden defects to the binding. Open the cover and check the front hinge and do the same for the rear hinge. Make sure that they are tight and not separating. See that the title page is present. Check for any signatures on the front free endpaper, half-title, and title page. If there are signatures, or inscriptions, see if they match the author's name, or that of another important figure. Fan the book while looking down the fore-edge and check to see if any pages have been removed. Fan the book a second time and watch for any marginal notes, highlighting or underlining. In my years of experience, I have yet to find any American dollars hidden between the pages. I have found several Italian lire which pre-dated the Second World War, though I've not followed up to see if they have any value. Sat-

isfied that the external and internal conditions are without exception, check the price guides for the author and title. If you find a citation for the book, be sure to read the entire entry to determine that the book you have in your hand matches the description of the one listed in the guide. A reprint of an early herbal without hand-colored botanical plates does not have the same value as the original. Record one-half to one-third of the listed value on the front free endpaper in the upper right corner in pencil. Remember to pay attention to the condition. As the condition begins to fall off, you should reduce the marked price by one eighth (1/8th) for each drop in the described condition. See the glossary (appendix VI) for descriptive terms, and read a few selected works in appendix I for further details.

Guidelines

There are some quick rule-of-thumb methods for arriving at prices without having to look each title up in a guide. Generally, American history or Americana published before 1950, in dust jackets as issued, will bring at least eight dollars and probably more at a general sale. The price guides are very good in this area and you should always check for a book in the Americana category. Americana includes American Indians, westward expansion, early American history and related topics. It is very popular and sells rapidly. Children's books are another hot area of interest. As the baby boomers age, they want the same books that they learned to read for their own children. Dick and Jane are now very collectible. Finding Dick and Jane readers in acceptable condition is not easy so the price at your sale could be as much as fifteen dollars. Pop-up books are those books dating from the 1930s that show a three-dimensional scene when you open the book. They are some of the most expensive children's titles when they can be found in fine condition. They command prices of $200 or more each, and are not easy to find. You'll

McCaffrey, Anne
- Decision at Doona. London: 1970. Dustwrapper (slightly rubbed).
  (Ellis) £40 [≃$71]
- Decision at Doona. London: 1970. Dustwrapper (slightly marked and rubbed). Signed by the author.
  (Susan Wood) £65 [≃$116]
- Dragondrums. London: 1979. Uncorrected proof copy. Wrappers. Signed by the author.
  (Susan Wood) £45 [≃$80]
- Pegasus in Flight. London: 1991. Dustwrapper. Signed by the author.
  (Susan Wood) £15 [≃$27]
- To Ride Pegasus. London: 1974. Dustwrapper (slightly creased, nicked and rubbed). Signed by the author.
  (Susan Wood) £50 [≃$89]

MacCaig, Norman
- Far Cry. London: 1943. Wrappers (very slightly marked and dusty, spine ends very slightly split, spine nicked). Author's 1st book.   *(Ulysses Bookshop)* £80 [≃$142]
- Midnights. Poem of the Month Club: 1970. Broadsheet. Signed by the author.
  (Ulysses Bookshop) £30 [≃$53]

McCammon, Robert R.
- The Night Boat. London: Kinnell, 1990. 1st hardcover edition. Dustwrapper.
  (Levin) $37.50 [≃£21]
- Swan Song. Arlington Heights: Dark Harvest, 1989. 1st hardcover edition, lettered state. One of 52 signed by the author. Wooden slipcase. No dustwrapper issued.
  (Levin) $450 [≃£253]

McCarthy, Cormac
- Blood Meridian. New York: Random House, (1985). Advance review copy with slip and photo laid in. Dustwrapper.
  (Between the Covers) $85 [≃£48]
- Suttree. New York: Random House, (1979). Uncorrected proof copy. Wrappers.
  (Between the Covers) $185 [≃£104]
- Suttree. New York: Random House, (1979). Remainder mark top edge. Dustwrapper.
  (Between the Covers) $50 [≃£28]

McCarthy, Mary
- Birds of America. Franklin Library: 1981. Leather gilt. Signed by the author.
  (Polyanthos) $50 [≃£28]
- The Oasis. New York: Random House, 1949. Dustwrapper.   *(Nouveau)* $60 [≃£34]

MacClanahan, Ed
- The Natural Man. London: Cape, 1983. 1st British edition. Dustwrapper. Author's 1st book.   *(Alphabet)* $35 [≃£20]

McClure, James
- The Caterpillar Cop. London: Gollancz, 1972. Dustwrapper, fine.
  (Mordida) $65 [≃£37]
- The Steam Pig. London: Gollancz, 1971. Small stamp on pastedown. Dustwrapper, fine.   *(Mordida)* $85 [≃£48]

McClure, Michael
- The Adept. New York: Delacorte, [1971]. Uncorrected proof copy. Spiral bound wrappers.   *(Dermont)* $75 [≃£42]

McCoy, Horace
- They Shoot Horses Don't They. New York: 1935. Spine very lightly sunned and slightly cocked. Dustwrapper (rubbed, slightly frayed). Author's 1st book.
  (Blakeney) £225 [≃$401]

McCullers, Carson
- Clock Without Hands. London: The Cresset Press, 1961. 1st English edition. Dustwrapper.   *(Chapel Hill)* $55 [≃£31]
- The Member of the Wedding. Boston: Houghton Mifflin, 1946. Some soiling and spine darkening. Dustwrapper. Signed by the author.   *(Between the Covers)* $875 [≃£492]
- The Mortgaged Heart. Boston: Houghton Mifflin, 1971. Dustwrapper (spine a little sunned).   *(Chapel Hill)* $30 [≃£17]
- Reflections in a Golden Eye. Boston: Houghton Mifflin, 1941. Advance review copy with photo laid in. 1st issue dustwrapper, fine.
  (Between the Covers) $450 [≃£253]
- The Square Root of Wonderful. Boston: Houghton Mifflin, 1958. Dustwrapper (extremities slightly rubbed, tiny chip rear panel).   *(Between the Covers)* $65 [≃£37]

McCullough, Colleen
- Tim. London: Angus & Robertson, 1975. Dustwrapper. Author's 1st book.
  (Nouveau) $50 [≃£28]

McCutcheon, George Barr
- Anderson Crow Detective. New York: Dodd, Mead, 1920. Dustwrapper. Fine.
  (Horowitz) $350 [≃£197]

MacDiarmid, Hugh
- The Fire of the Spirit. Glasgow: Duncan Glen, 1965. One of 350 numbered. Wrappers.   *(Antic Hay)* $45 [≃£25]
- In Memoriam James Joyce. London: 1955.

Figure Two: Price Guide. Example page from *Modern First Editions, Annual Register of Book Values*, edited by Michael Cole, The Clique, 1992, p.132.

have to decide whether you want to staff a special table at the sale for the "better" books, giving the local supporters of your organization the first crack at them, or go right to the specialists.

Some will balk at these prices, because they have seen sales where all hard-bound books are two dollars and paperback 25¢. Those days have changed. Even garage sales now price hard-covers at five dollars and new paperbacks at a dollar. Books are expensive these days, and people want to recoup a better portion of what might have been a $25 initial outlay. Your organization's fund-raising efforts are for a most worthy cause—the continued support of public programs. The customers at your event are still receiving a bargain price and partici-pating in a civic function at the same time.

Paperbacks

Don't jump to the conclusion that only hard-cover books can be valuable. Many paperbacks stored for years in attics and then donated will amaze you not only for their value, but also by how quickly they will disappear. In some instances the true first edition of a book was in paperback. For your own education, see if you can dis-cover the identity of Richard Bachman who wrote such titles as *Thinner, The Long Walk,* and *Roadwork*. These paperbacks were originally published at $3.95. Today they sell for $40 and up, based on their con-dition. Don't immediately assume that because the book is a paperback, that it is not collectible or desirable to the right per-son.

Magazines

Magazines may bring looks of terror to the faces of book sale organizers. Magazines are heavy, they take even more time to sort than books, and often don't sell. Too many times you'll be deluged with the *National Geographic* and the *Smithsonian,* none of which are older than last year. The only *National Geographics* that have much

value are those published before 1914. *Smithsonian* is a wonderful magazine, but the only person who asks if you have any at the sale will already have all the issues you received as donations.

Magazines with Norman Rockwell cover illustrations are of great interest, as are issues of *Life* and *Look*, which are signifi-cant to various people because a particular publication date relates to a memorable occasion in their life, or the issue contains an article by an author they might collect. Many authors who are now important liter-ary figures received their start as short story writers for magazines. E. B. White of *Char-lotte's Web* fame earned his living as a writer for *New Yorker* magazine. Books of his collected columns still sell today. Find-ing a magazine with a signed article by White would be a major coup. It would def-initely be a candidate for your better books table. The January through March issues of *Look* for 1967 are of great interest because they contain William Manchester's first installments of *Death of a President*. Peo-ple often pay $100 or more for the four issues in fine condition. If you want a real shock, check the reverse of the title page and see which magazines first featured all of the short stories in Stephen King's *Night Shift*.

The best magazines are those containing how-to information written for craftpersons and hobbyists. People are always seeking to assemble complete collections of maga-zines. They do not necessarily need all of the issues to learn a particular handicraft, but there is a natural human tendency toward seeking completeness.

Keep an eye open for the first issue of any magazine. Somewhere, someone wants that issue and will pay more than 25¢ for it. As before, remember that condition is impor-tant, and that magazines are no exception. If the cover is missing, pages are torn and stained, then it's just as well to put it in the stack with the discarded and unsold maga-zines at the conclusion of the sale.

Some popular magazines to watch for are *Mother Earth News, Organic Gardening, Guns and Ammo, Field and Stream*, as well as the popular weeklies of the 1960s.

Recordings

Recordings are often received as donations for fund-raising sales. You're on your own here. Try to find a volunteer who is very interested in music to assist you. Record condition is even more important than book condition because of the nature of the medium. A book in good condition can still be enjoyed, but a record in only good condition will annoy a listener with the snap, crackle hiss and pop of the scratches.

Price guide limitations

In all cases of price checking, one item of advice you must consider very carefully is that price guides are just that— guides. They do not necessarily reflect what a book brought between a willing buyer and a willing seller. In some instances a guide will provide a range. This takes into account matters of condition, provenance, desirability, collectibility and rarity. Many times you are not privy to the background information that allowed the specialists to reach their estimate of value. Your copy may appear to be the same, but lack a specific detail. Geographic location can also affect the price of a book. In Chicago, the published history of a small county in Nebraska will not have much value, but the price guide may list $250 for the volume. Even on the "better" books table, the odds of selling that book, even to a professional bookseller for $100 are slim. Someone sold the volume, perhaps, for the price guide sum, but they also probably sold it to a person in that Nebraska county who had spent a great deal of time searching for their county history. Price guides must be used with the listing bookseller in mind. The better guides will provide the name of the bookseller who sold the book, and before assigning a price to the book, it is important to check the appendix to find where the bookseller operates. New York prices are higher than most of those in the Midwest, while the prices for West Coast books tend to be some of the most expensive in the country. These are generalizations only and are not intended to offend, it's just a tendency I have noticed over the years. If you intend to price books and expect people to pay a bit more for them, you need to do your work carefully.

Auction records can also be misleading. All of the details of a book's condition will not be forthcoming, though you will know who bought the book. Unless you become very familiar with members of the rare and out-of-print book trade, the names will not mean much to you, and won't be much help in assessing if the price paid was high, low or average. In many instances auction records will not contain records for books that sold for less than $50. If you combine that knowledge with the other price guides, and don't find a book you have listed anywhere, then there is a strong possibility that the book is not particularly valuable, desirable or collectible. Does your organization have the time to find the one person in the world ready to pay five dollars for it?

Many price guides will include information useful in determining important information about a book. Points of issue may be listed, and what appeared at first to be the first edition of Stephen Crane's *The Little Regiment* may lack the required six pages of advertisements in the back of the book with the headline reading "Gilbert Parker's Best Books." Even though the dust jacket is present for this 1896 beauty, the latter impression of the first edition will probably only bring $200 rather than $400.

Remember that in many price guides, the assembled prices have been gleaned from bookseller's catalogs. The bookseller may be the best in the world at one particular subject, and their catalog reflects that expertise in high prices of ultra quality collectible and even rare books, while another bookseller has an open shop of general used books and issues an occasional catalog. Both will be listed in the price guide, one with books that you'll probably not ever see nor have a ready customer for, while the other's general knowledge may lead them to price a signed, limited edition Stephen King at $25 only because they can't stand the man or his genre.

With general price guides, remember that there is no way of knowing that a book listed actually sold for the catalog price, and that's what is listed in the guide. Perhaps a prospective customer offered less for the book and the bookseller, recognizing that it had been around the shop at $25 for two years, gratefully accepted $15. The price guide will still show that book at $25. Perhaps the bookseller read a reference work on Stephen King and quickly changed the price of the book to $350 after realizing the mistake. The price guide will still show $25. So, the guides must be taken for what they are. They are guides, not set-in-stone information that can be held as the one and only benchmark of value.

As you begin to find booksellers who specialize in given subjects, it might be a good idea to write and request one of their catalogs. These catalogs offer a quick way to see the price trends, especially for those booksellers who deal in one particular subject. Always include two dollars to help defray the bookseller's printing and postage expenses. I can promise you that a bookseller will remember your courteous and professional gesture.

In appendix III are a number of useful general and several very specific guides to pricing used and out-of-print books. Many are still in print and available for sale. They can often be found in the reference section of larger city and university libraries. You could send a volunteer with several questions you might have about potential "better" books to those reference collections every few weeks, if you wish to save the expense of purchase. Most will not be

available for interlibrary loan, so it is best to take your questions of value and go to the reference source.

The volumes of *Books in Print* also serve as useful pricing tools. If a recent book cannot be found in any of the various price guides, you can always check to see if it is still in-print or not. In-print books are available without much trouble, and places like Sam's Warehouse often carries books for 50% off the cover price, so you'll have to price in-print volumes accordingly. If you find the book to be out-of-print, price according to the desirability of the book's subject in your immediate area. Remember that many popular topics have out-of-print titles that are going up in value. All too often a hobbyist or collector will procrastinate about the purchase of a book only to find that when they finally get around to buying, the store is out of stock and the publisher has declared it out-of-print. That person tells another person involved in the same hobby about the book's unavailability, and now there are two people interested in a book that is no longer available in the normal market place. Such is the way that books increase in value.

Using Experts

Another method of pricing books involves doing what you can with your volunteer work force, pricing the various boxes of sorted books, then calling a local professional bookseller, special collections librarian, or the local librarian. They will be able to check the work of your pricers. Be kind to the professionals that come to help. Advise them that you need assistance checking your prices. Tell them that they will not be able to buy at this time, but that you will extend them an invitation to the member's preview. Ask them to assist your sale with a donation of their time. Advise them that the books have been sorted and priced, and that you want them to check your work and pick out any valuable books that might have been missed for the "better books" table at the sale. If there are several booksellers in your area, pay a personal call on each of them, and ask what they consider to be their strengths. Then invite them to donate a review of your pricing in those particular areas.

There is another gray area that will create an uproar among my colleagues, but it needs attention. If several specialist booksellers review the work of your pricing crews and one or more of the booksellers finds a gem of a book, *let them buy it.* But never, ever tell them that such a possibility exists in advance. They must verify that the price they are willing to pay is fair and equitable, that is, 60% of any listed entry in a price guide. You cannot allow them to strip you of all the valuable books, but a book worth $200 will probably not sell for $75 at your event, and if you can receive $125 for it in advance I would advise you to take the money.

You may in the future wish to work on a regular basis with the local booksellers, giving individual specialists an equal opportunity to work with you on the book sales. Avoid favoritism, for the bad publicity will spread like a brushfire and severely limit your donations should patrons discover that there's a black market book business afoot in your organization. You can work with the local bookshops by keeping an eye open for books within their specialty. Every bookseller has a few books that they especially desire. It won't be too much additional effort to warn your volunteers to watch for those titles.

It is important to raise as much money as possible with the donations that you receive. If a book is donated that your research confirms to be especially valuable, say $400, what are the odds that a customer will purchase that book at your sale for $100? You would be better off if you called a specialist for that book and offer it to them at 75% of the assessed market value. You would not be giving them an unfair advantage; you are earning the most revenue for your organization.

Never allow booksellers to "pick" over the titles for an upcoming sale. Their skimming off the cream will certainly become common knowledge and hurt the prospects of the book sale. Only offer uncommon and expensive titles to booksellers selected for their expertise on a given subject or author. Be certain of the edition, condition and price before calling or writing.

There is an additional incentive that I will relate when working with booksellers and cultivating relationships with them. When working with the local professionals, have the books that you want examined on a table, out of the box and ready for examination. Stay a box or so ahead of them, returning the scrutinized titles back into the appropriate box when they start on the next one. I know that this is handling the books one additional time, but it is a great way of learning value. It would be a good idea to have your volunteers available to watch this process, as it will be a valuable experience in pricing.

Pricing alternatives

There is one last procedure of pricing books for the sale, which entails two alternatives. Organizations that receive tremendous numbers of donations often find that it is the only way they can keep up with the flow of books. The first alternative has the volunteer group sort the books as they arrive into subject categories, and as they do so, pricing each hardback book at three dollars and each paperback at a dollar. Attempts can be made to check on books that appear to be of value, but on the whole, the emphasis is on pricing the books consistently in an effort to make them all equal candidates for purchase. Even with this method, you can contact the area professionals and ask them to check the few books that you pulled as possible exceptions.

The other alternative is not to sort any of the books except by paperback and hard-back. Each hard-cover tome is priced at three dollars and paperbacks are one dollar, as they are placed on the tables. People can have the times of their lives hunting for the scattered treasures. This method is ideal for large and small sales alike when the number of volunteers is very limited. The only caveat is the amount of space you need between the aisles, as people have a tendency to bunch up in sales where the books are tabled in an unsorted fashion.

If you are too careful in pricing, and make the sale a miniature used bookshop in time and space, you'll be left with a good number of books for next year's sale. You do not want to rebox books, store them, and bring them out again another year. You and the sale sponsor should know the tastes of your local clientele. With that in mind, price the books so they will sell, but at the same time, don't give them away if you've taken the time to research those which you know to have a better value than three dollars each.

Types of books

Associated with the concept of price are words you need to know in relation to the commodity. Out-of-print, collectible, scarce and rare are important and often confusing designations. Each is descriptive of a type of book in all of the various categories or subjects. Used is any book in any condition, in-print and out-of-print. Used books abound in many subjects and often, that's what you'll receive as donations. Many people wait too long to buy a book and discover that it is out-of-print. That means that bookstores and the publishers are both out of stock with no immediate plans to republish the book in the future. In that case, the person wanting the book must inquire of a used and out-of-print book-seller whether their shop might have a copy, or the customer can attend book sales in the hopes that the wayward volume can be found.

A collectible book is one that has been out-of-print or was issued in an edition smaller than the immediate demand for the book. A good example is the Charles Addams cartoon books. I believe there are six or seven volumes of his collected cartoons. Originally published at $3.50 in the 1950s they now command $40 to $70 each with signed copies reaching prices of $200. Movies can bring forgotten books back into fashion! When sorting and pricing, don't forget to watch for sleepers like Charles Addams. They're collectible.

Scarce books are those that are often found in the price guides. They are books in any subject, are any age from 1500 to the present, and are in demand by a number of people. An example is Richard Brautigan's *A Confederate General from Big Sur*. Published in 1964, it is not easy to find and everyone who collects Brautigan wants a copy. Hence the price runs to $200 or more. Just think what you could pencil in for the price if the book were signed by the author!

A rare book is one that everyone would like to find, few can afford and only one copy comes onto the market every few years. Any number of conditions can make a book rare. There were few copies produced, few survived because the book was thought unimportant at the time, or the book contained handsome illustrations and was cut up for framing. One such book is John J. Audubon's *The Birds of America*. Drawn and produced between 1828 and 1837, there were 87 parts issued in original paper wrappers or covers. There are very few copies available, and with millionaires being made every minute in America, more and more people would like to acquire such a rarity. If a copy of this beautiful work with its 435 colored plates of birds were to sell today, it would bring over one million dollars. I doubt that any of your sales will find such a book, but you never can totally rule out the possibility. Do your home work and see what you can discover about an unassuming little pamphlet called *Tamerlane* by an American poet and author named Edgar Allen Poe.

Finally, age does not make a book valuable. There are many books from the 1500s on numerous religious subjects that can be bought for $50 or less. Condition applies to any book regardless of age. Condition is important for a book's price. New books can be very valuable, given the right subject, an early author who later makes it big, like King, Clancy, or Cannell. And finally, don't be afraid to price a book a few dollars higher the first time around. Someone at the book sale will pick it up, hold it, put it down, then decide that they would be happier owning the book now, rather than let the next person in line pick it up, so they'll pay the price, support the Friends of the Library group and perhaps, bring the book back in several months as a donation for next year's sale.

6

First Editions

Invariably, I'll be talking with an individual about their books, and they will tell me they are certain that they have a first edition of Walt Whitman's *Leaves of Grass*. This will lead me to ask when the book was published and the name of the publisher. If they aren't certain of the details, we will find the book on their shelf. It's usually a well-worn copy, with the contents loose and falling out of the binding. In checking the title page I notice that the publisher is Altemus, located in Philadelphia, and the book was published in 1899. I know that the first edition (i.e., the first time a book appears in print) for Whitman's *Leaves of Grass* appeared in 1855 in Brooklyn, New York. I try to explain the difference between the two books, but I am usually met with a blank look. They are certain that the book they have is valuable. Nearly everyone has heard of first editions and uses the words to describe every book they have ever known.

Some of the most often asked questions in the area of used, out-of-print, and collectible books are about first editions, how to tell if you have a first edition, and whether a first edition is always valuable.

People collect first editions because they represent the first published record of an author's ideas. The term first edition applies to all of the subjects in books. There are first editions of children's books, for western Americana, geology, even cookbooks. Any subject you can think of has first editions.

Identifying first editions

How to tell if a book in your possession is a first edition is another matter entirely. In most cases, a first edition will have a date on the reverse of the title page that matches the date on the front of the title page. In many cases, not only will the two dates agree, but there may also be the printed statement "First Edition" under the date or at the bottom of the reverse side of the title page, which is often called the copyright page.

It is not always enough to have the two dates in agreement. You must check further to determine if what you have is the first edition, first printing, or a later impression of the first edition. Usually, underneath the publisher information on the reverse of the title page you will find a series of numbers or letters. A first edition, first impression will have the numbers 1 through 10, while those with letters will be a through j, often in small case. When the numbers and letters begin to change, you'll be able to recognize later printings. Even if the two dates on the title page agree, but the numbers start with 3 and run through 12, you know that the book you have is the first edition, third printing. Likewise, title page identical dates for front and rear with letters c through l shows that the book is also the third printing.

When changes to the text are such that there must be new typesetting and page alterations, a second edition of the work is published. Often, a new date on the front of the title page will be printed, with the original date on the reverse of the title page. Many times the words "second edition" are also present on the reverse.

Many publishers are consistent with their identification of their own first editions, but very few publishers use the identical method to signify the first edition of a book. There are two titles in appendix I that deal specifically with a publisher's method of first edition identification. Boutell and Zemple's books are excellent starting points for learning about the subject.

On occasion, a book will be published in a small quantity by a non-mainstream publisher as the first edition. Then, the book becomes an instant hit, the rights are sold to a major New York publisher, and another printing of the book appears. The new printing by the major publisher may conspicuously say first edition, but it is only the first edition by that particular publisher. The true first edition was the small press run by the small publisher. One such example is Tom Clancy's *Hunt for Red October.* It was originally published in a very limited press run by the Naval Institute Press at Annapolis, Maryland in 1984. Putnam brought out the trade edition in 1985, and it rocketed to an instant bestseller.

There are thousands of first editions available in used and out-of-print bookstores that are not particularly valuable. Their publication price may have been $19.95,

but today they are often found on shelves for five dollars or less, with duplicates available at every turn. First editions are valuable when the book becomes collectible, with people buying it faster than copies are available or when the book is out-of-print and a demand develops for it.

Modern first editions

Modern first editions is a collecting category apart from all other subjects. It is an area that defies easy description, and a group of ten booksellers would each have their own distinct definition of the term. To me, modern first editions are those works of fiction published during the twentieth century. I would go even further and say that modern first editions can be divided into three groups: literature such as Faulkner, Hemingway, London, and others; turn-of-the-century fiction; and present day fiction consisting of mysteries and detective stories by authors such as Sanders, Cannell and Lee Smith. You could spend a year organizing and re-ordering your lists of such books.

Many individuals collect all the first editions of one writer they like, a sometimes formidable task if the writer became famous after their fifteenth book and the first ten have been out-of-print for eight years. Others assemble collections of the first edition of an author's first book and move on, trying to assemble a cross section of modern fiction. Still others collect only Newbery, Caldecott or Pulitzer prize-winning fiction. One of the best ways to learn the price of first editions is to contact Patricia and Allen Ahearn at Quill and Brush (PO Box 5365, Rockville, MD 20848). They issue an amazing array of modern author price guides. Write to them for more information.

It is important to understand that there are many reprint houses active in the publishing world. Reprint houses buy the rights to a book and then issue it in a different format, often on lesser quality paper and in a

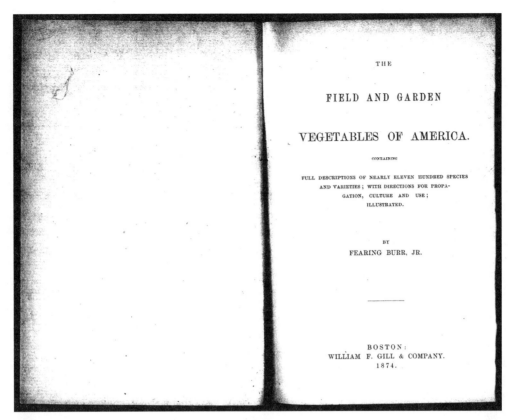

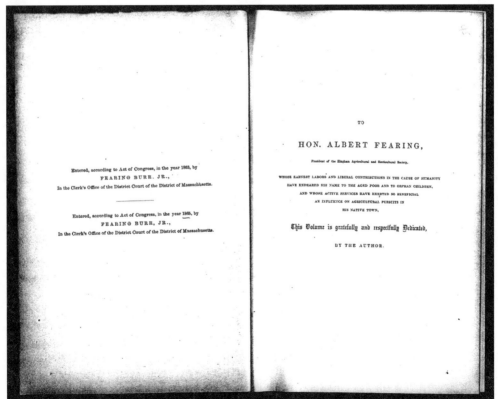

Figure Three: Example of a Later Printing. Note in this example that the title page indicates the book was published in 1874, but it was originally copyrighted in 1863 and 1865.

less expensive binding in an effort to reach the mass market. During the early days of the twentieth century until about 1950, reprints were more common than they are today. The important imprints to look for are Grossett and Dunlap, Collier, A. L. Burt, World and Altemus. There were very few first editions issued by these publishers, and you will often find them associated with some very collectible authors and titles. A. L. Burt published the Tarzan series by Edgar Rice Burroughs, Grossett and Dunlap did the Zane Grey western series, and Altemus was known for the literature it produced. Part of your education for your book sale might come from visiting an out-of-print bookseller to scan their shelves to learn price trends. You may occasionally see some of the reprints mentioned above, with full first edition value attached to them. We both know the titles in question were acquired early in the bookseller's career, and they are kept around as a reminder of inexperience, right?

Other collectible editions

In addition to first editions, there are several different types of published works that may be more collectible. They are limited editions, autographed editions, and specially bound copies.

The limited edition may be a first edition, but the distinguishing factor is that a predetermined number of copies were printed. Either the particular subject was perceived to be of limited interest or the book design or method of printing and binding gives it a special collectible value. In some publishing circles today there is a belief that a limited edition may impart a greater sense of collectible quality to a book. Be sure that you don't put a heavy price on a book because of a stated limitation. Generally you will find the limitation notice at the end of the volume as a fly leaf or facing side of the rear free endpaper. Books limited to 1000 copies are not particularly limited,

unless there are a great many more individuals than that anxious for the book.

Two good examples of limited editions are Stephen King's *Dolan's Cadillac* and *Cycle of the Werewolf.* Both had short press runs for limited editions, and both were signed and are now very expensive. *Dolan's Cadillac* had a printing in a limited edition of 250 copies signed by Mr. King, and four of the 250 copies were bound in a special leather binding. Copies of that particular specially bound, signed limited edition reach prices of $500. The same book without the special binding has been sold for $150. Such is the world of collectible books. *Cycle of the Werewolf* had a limitation of 350 copies which were signed by the author, and these copies sell for $300 and more. Remember though, that the first trade editions of his works still sell for their original cover price when they are still in print, and that his new editions are so popular that the first edition has an extremely high press run.

Autograph editions are normally those which are signed by the author in an agreement with the publisher. It is a promotional device to create demand for a book. The signed book makes the owner feel that the author took special care with a particular book. Books signed by an important historical figure will make a book more desirable to a collector, but even the autographed edition of Gustavaf Geijerstam's *My Boy*, published in 1933, will not make it a valuable book.

Special bindings

As I pointed out with Stephen King, there are special bindings that enhance the value of a book. These books are often from a small publisher, where most of the books are bound in one form, with the special copies bound and limited to individuals who assisted with the production of the book. If the main press run of the book is to be paperback, then a suitable number, such as ten, may be bound in cloth as gifts for

Figure 4: Example of a Signed Limited Edition.

The Sterling Morton Library Bibliographies
in
Botany and Horticulture

III

Benjamin Smith Barton
and
William Paul Crillon Barton

Ian MacPhail

Ian MacPhil

The Morton Arboretum, 1986

*Frontispieces: Benjamin Smith Barton: Portrait by Charles B. J. F. de Saint Mémin.
Engraved by Christian Gobrecht and published originally in The Port folio,
series 4, 1: 273 (1816). William Paul Crillon Barton: Photograph copied
from the Jane Loring Gray Album, Gray Herbarium, Harvard University.
Courtesy of the Hunt Institute for Botanical Documentation.*

Copyright 1986 by The Morton Arboretum, Lisle, Illinois 60532

Edition: 300 copies

Composition: Typoservice Corporation
Printing: The Meriden Gravure Company

Design: Nancy S. Hart

those involved with bringing the book into the world. It is difficult to know if the book was specially bound by the publisher when the book was produced, or if a bibliophile had the book specially bound after it was purchased. The purist collector could assist you in determining if a binding was applied at a later date, because often the original paperback cover will be bound in with the original contents in the new binding. Even if a book is signed, limited and specially bound, it is no guarantee of value. The subject may be of limited interest, and the value will not ever reach a level beyond its published price.

Other factors

First editions, and all of the other variations on the issue of an edition require that there be a well-known author, (or one with a future), an interesting subject, or be from a famous publisher known for their taste and technique in the production of books.

Besides the first edition, books are collected by people because they are by an author the collector admires or enjoys. Surrounding themselves with that individual's books may make the collector feel closer to the author. Collections are also developed on any number of subjects beyond those which you sorted for the sale. One of my friends collects books on croquet. Another collects books on bird decoys of the Eastern Seaboard. If you can imagine a subject, then there is likely someone who collects books in that field. Finally, some individuals and institutions collect books by a single publisher. One such example is the Meriden-Stinehour Press. They produce a number of the limited edition works for institutions and private libraries and have an understanding of paper grain, book design and composition as well as binding quality. Their books are beautifully designed and produced, and they will pass the test of time.

7

Working With Booksellers

Booksellers are individuals with a deep abiding appreciation for the printed word. They feel most at ease when surrounded by their friends—books. A bookseller will talk endlessly about books they might have had, the collection that got away, or how they found their one most treasured and rare book. Just as there are any number of collectors in as many subjects, the same is true for the people who buy and sell books. I am most concerned with the used, out-of-print and rare bookseller for the purposes of the book sale. Those booksellers who specialize in really rare books may not be the best ones to contact for assistance with the sale, but never leave any stone unturned. Stranger things have happened. Folks may call a rare bookseller asking if they are interested in buying a collection of marble books, and learn that the bookshop only specializes in fishing books published before 1850. However, the bookseller could refer the caller to a local library friends group and suggest donating the collection to their next book sale. Any contact with the professional trade can't hurt.

Many booksellers with a general used book trade are hounded by potential customers eager to turn their unwanted volumes into ready cash. Rather than turn them away

dejected, a cooperative bookseller who knows about your next sale may be willing to tell the frustrated customer that the local friends of the library or similar group is sponsoring a sale to raise funds, and that donations are now being accepted.

Recruiting booksellers

When working with booksellers, don't be afraid to ask them for help, appeal to them as the experts, show them that you recognize they support worthy causes in the community. This can be of mutual benefit. If a neophyte collector finds two or three titles by an author they are just beginning to like, then the next step should be a referral to the professional bookseller for guidance and assistance in collection development. Your organization and the bookseller both have a stake in the future.

After your first sale, you should not be surprised by the wealth of knowledge you will accrue about books. You and your volunteers probably fielded questions about all types of books. The public will know that your organization did an effective job in selling their unwanted books, and this should result in a regular stream of donated titles in the future.

Knowing local booksellers as well as you do, you'll want to be a regular visitor or caller, telling them what's coming in that might interest them. If it is the policy of your sponsoring organization, you may want to offer special titles to them in advance of the sale. Pricing is a key consideration under these circumstances. Establish a price which is reasonable enough to allow the bookseller to make a fair profit and keep a deserving customer happy. It will still be more than the price you would receive at the sale.

What if there are no general used booksellers in your area? What if the good and better books that arrive all year are not of interest to the local professionals? In many cases your donors may have visited their shop in an effort to turn their books into cash and found themselves turned away. Under those conditions, how do you turn good books into cash and develop a continuing source of profit for your organization?

Reaching a national market

One alternative is to learn how to quote books for sale to booksellers around the country. This is a lot of work and requires dedication, but it is a profitable sideline that should be considered. It only takes some knowledge and some postcards to offer books for sale to booksellers throughout the nation. For this, you'll find the books wanted list in the *Bookquote* and *AB Bookman's Weekly* valuable. In these publications are lists of specific books wanted by booksellers. It will take some time to scan the pages of the books wanted, but soon you'll know which booksellers are looking for particular subjects. You can sell the right books to them if you keep your eyes open.

In addition to the books wanted section, there are also pages of books for sale. These pages will help you learn more about the prices the retail market will pay for books. Though your organization's event is

more of a wholesale affair, you'll still be able to offer select titles at higher prices as they cross the sorting tables. Understand that you'll not be generating more than a few postcards each month. The really good books, some of which I have described, don't turn up all that often.

Describing condition

Knowing how to assess condition, evaluate price, and with the knowledge of what subjects are of interest, you'll be able to generate a quote to a bookseller that they will know came from a person who knows books. I receive quotes daily in my business and I can quickly tell who knows how to describe a book's condition and who doesn't. Even if a book is inexpensive compared to its potential sales price to a collector, I'll probably not purchase it if the seller's postcard stumbles, falters, or misuses the conventional words describing the book's condition. Nothing is worse than having to send a book back because the condition, edition and details were wrong.

Be careful in your descriptions. If the book has color illustrations, check the number to see that it is correct. If you call a local bookseller and inform them that you found a fine color plate book, and then you both discover that two of the required plates are absent, you will waste your own time, and your relationship with the bookseller might be adversely affected. Carefully check the pages to see that none have been written on, removed or otherwise defaced, and that the hinges and joints are tight. Once you are satisfied that the book is right, research the price and then give the local bookseller a call. It's best to take more than one book at time for their review and possible purchase. Remember not to run all of your great finds by your booksellers. Some will be needed for the special table at the next book sale. When you visit the bookseller, arrange your books from the least interesting and valuable to the one real blockbuster you might have for last. It helps with the impact of the selection and adds to the fun of the moment. The bookseller will relish the surprise.

If you decide to offer a book to a professional elsewhere in the nation, supply the bookseller with all the essential information. Provide the author, title, place of publication, publisher, date published, number of pages, and type of binding. If cloth, state whether a dust jacket is present. Describe the condition of the dust jacket, cloth binding and the contents. Be conservative in your descriptions to avoid any unpleasant surprises. Always state a price, including postage or shipping. If you have set the price too high, and the bookseller is interested, there is a good chance that they may make a counter-offer. Be open to suggestions.

Finding specialties

Try to become familiar with the publications for booksellers. Your local library may already receive them. Two of the publications in appendix I are your ticket to finding and working with booksellers around the country. *Antiquarian, Specialty, and Used Book Sellers* by James and Karen Ethridge provide a state-by-state listing of booksellers. The information is arranged alphabetically by state, with details on specialty subjects in the bookshop, hours, and whether they issue a catalog. You might even be astounded to learn that there is a specialist bookseller living right under your nose, that you've never heard about. Many booksellers who only buy and sell one subject work through the mail with catalogues, and rarely advertise locally. They often have a wealth of information about both general and specialty books. It would be very worth your while to make an appointment to meet with them and ask them to serve in an advisory capacity for your book sale event.

Another essential reference for locating booksellers is the *AB Bookman's Yearbook*. It contains articles, advertisements and appendices with addresses for auction houses, appraisal services, specialty publishers and university presses. In addition, booksellers are listed by state and city as well as by specialty. This publication is particularly important because it will help you to establish relationships with regional booksellers around the country. The regional groups of booksellers often produce publications advertising their membership. The organizations exist in the Midwest, Northeast, upstate New York and in the Pacific Northwest, to name a few. If you do not locate a bookseller nearby in either Ethridge or *AB*, then get in contact with the nearest regional organization and ask for their help.

The organizational directories offer a broader look at those specialists who conduct business either by mail or in an open shop, but are not often found in the normal course of business. From the regional list you should be able to locate some civic-minded person to assist you with your fund-raising event.

Bookseller relations

There is always the problem of offending one bookseller because you asked a local competitor to assist in the sale first. Make a blanket offer to all those involved locally in the book trade to participate in an advisory capacity. Keep no secrets about the sale and the quality of books that are received. Those who choose not to participate and then regret their decision will have no one to blame but themselves.

Another alternative is to assemble the local booksellers and ask them whether they would be willing to determine the participating bookseller by lot. If so have them draw slips from a hat passed among them. Mark one with a black spot in advance. Whoever gets the black spot is the person to serve on the book sale committee. For obvious reasons, Robert Louis Stevenson would like the irony in this! Repeat the drawing each year, with the previous year's volunteer ineligible for the drawing. Another alternative would be to number the slips, and let that establish the rotation for service. That way, the local booksellers will all have an equal chance to participate and perhaps garner some publicity for their own enterprise.

8
Cultivating Donations

Conducting a successful book sale requires that you have some books that can stimulate the interest of the local media beyond just another charitable function. You should make every effort to solicit donations for the "better" books table at the sale from booklovers or others in the community who are in a position to help.

Perhaps you can even "seed" the "better" books with a donation or two from your local professional booksellers or their regional friends. If you can begin to establish the idea that the book sale is more than just another fund-raising opportunity, but is also an important event that will improve equipment and services for your library or other local service organization, people will make an extra effort to participate.

Often, it is the same folks in town who are approached for donations of money for civic functions. They may be intrigued if they're asked to donate a special book rather than money. It might lead them to ask more about the event. Inform them of your need for special books that will be used to draw attention to the sale. Explain that other titles will probably be found that have greater value as well, but that every better book will aid in gaining media coverage.

Don't just limit yourself to one better book. Ask the community leaders who have many books if they can help you to identify others who collect books. A phone call or introduction would be of great value. Since people who love books are always eager to talk books, you'll probably receive an invitation to drop by and see their collections. Take the opportunity to mention the upcoming book sale. Ask them if they are interested in participating. If they are unable to volunteer their time, ask if they might have some duplicate titles or other books that they have outgrown. You might be pleasantly pleased with the donations you can obtain through this strategy. If you're told to give them some time to think about a donation, be sure to follow through within a week's time. They'll know that you are serious. Offer to come by and pick up the books for them. Whenever a gift of books is received, be certain to keep the details confidential, unless the donor wants recognition. No telling whose feelings might be hurt if the source of a large lot of books was known.

Tax-deductibility

Avoid discussion about the tax-deductibility of the book donation. Before the donor could claim a deduction for the present value of a book that is donated to your organization, you would have to keep the book for a minimum period of two years before you would be free to sell it. The donor would not be able to claim any accumulated appreciation on the book as a deduction. If you received the book as a donation and sold it soon after, then the donor could only deduct the basis value, that is, what they originally paid for the book. All of this is based on the assumption that your group is classified as a charitable organization under Section 501(c)(3) of the Internal Revenue Code.

Appraisal

I would doubt that you receive a donation so large that it would require an appraisal. But if you did, you need to know that it is the donor's responsibility to furnish the appraisal. You might suggest qualified professional booksellers who could conduct an appraisal for the donor, but that is where your involvement ends. You should not enter into any negotiations on the value of any books to be donated. If an individual asks for a receipt, you can count, or have them count the number of books, paperbacks, magazines or records they donated, and then have the librarian or other officer of your organization sign and date the receipt as to the number and kinds of items donated.

The procedure becomes a little more complicated if a donation of books or other items for the book sale is over $5000. Meticulous records are required for the transaction. A very formal, written and annotated appraisal must be obtained by the donor, and then all the parties, including the appraiser, must sign IRS form 8283 documenting the donation. If you should ever receive such an unrestricted gift, it would be better, if possible, to hold it for a minimum of two years before even considering the sale of the item to raise funds. If an individual has those types of books, a direct gift of a wall of shelves or a library wing might be a better option!

9
Publicity

Advertising and publicity for the event are nearly as important as your volunteers. Contact the local newspapers and talk them into doing a feature story complete with photos. Let folks know some of the better books that will be available. Tell them about any special events that might be planned during the book sale, like an auction, or an author reading and signing party at the library. Any combination to keep the public's mind focused on the benefits of the sale to the library or the sponsoring organization is critical.

Posters around town are an effective method, and so are handbills placed in each book checked out of the library for two weeks prior to the sale. A direct mailing to the members of the friends group will also prove beneficial. Any checks taken during the sale should be held long enough to copy the personal data so a post card can be printed and sent a month before the same event in years to come. Direct mail is an often overlooked method of advertising nonprofit functions. If your mailing surpasses 250, and you plan to do other events or provide notification of library programs, then you might want to consider a bulk-rate permit. The local postal authorities can give you the details.

Using radio & TV

Don't just buy radio advertising time. Instead, offer to do some on-the-air interviews. Radio personalities are often anxious to have someone to talk with in their lonely booths. Encourage listeners with questions to call. Don't just contact the stations you know. Use the resources of the library and listen to the radio to pick as many stations as possible in the area. Request time on the air. Don't single out any one audience as a target. Everyone should be interested in the book sale.

You might even be able to record a short television segment on one of the public access channels available to communities with cable television. Show some of the interesting and unique items that will be offered in the sale. As always, stress how the library or sponsor will benefit from the proceeds.

Reaching a wider market

Two months before the sale, begin sending all of the booksellers in a 150 mile radius a post card. Send a post card every week until just before the sale. The booksellers

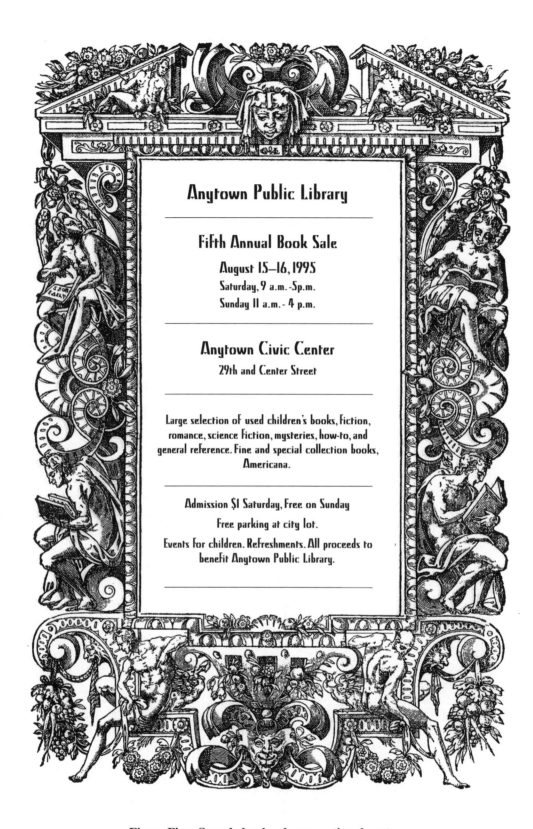

Anytown Public Library

Fifth Annual Book Sale

August 15–16, 1995
Saturday, 9 a.m.-5 p.m.
Sunday 11 a.m.- 4 p.m.

Anytown Civic Center
29th and Center Street

Large selection of used children's books, fiction, romance, science fiction, mysteries, how-to, and general reference. Fine and special collection books, Americana.

Admission $1 Saturday, Free on Sunday
Free parking at city lot.
Events for children. Refreshments. All proceeds to benefit Anytown Public Library.

Figure Five: Sample book sale promotional poster.

are often the ones who will buy books in quantity.

If you are in a large metropolitan area, arrange with the local hotels to have flyers for your sale placed with the publicity packets of each room. One place to turn to for assistance is the local chamber of commerce. They will be able to assist you in identifying and contacting the businesses with the resources to improve the sale. In larger communities, the convention and visitor's bureau will be a tremendous asset. Work with them a year in advance, in order to identify a weekend that has the least competition from other activities. Fund raising is a full-time occupation for many, and any competent free assistance has to be utilized.

Place posters in as many public buildings and locations as you can. Muster the volunteers to tour town. Mail your posters and advertising packets to towns up to 50 miles away, and ask the local librarian to post them for you. Tell the individual you'll be happy to do the same for them should the need arise.

Should you have a good selection of children's and young adult titles for the sale, consider sending a flyer home with each child at school. Books are expensive these days and if a parent knows that they can purchase good quality books for fair used prices, they will very often attend and let the child pick out a whopping stack of books.

Although it can be expensive, it might not hurt to advertise your sale in *AB Bookman, Firsts* magazine or *Bookquote*. Provide an address where interested individuals can write for more information. You can use the library's or your organization's address for receiving any inquiries about the sale. Be sure to have information available on local accommodations for out-of-town attendees.

Building a mailing list

Keep track of the number of people in attendance at your sale. It can be used to solicit memberships, and to generate a mailing list for future sales. You can tell the public in your publicity that there will be a free drawing for a particular book. To participate, they only need to supply their name and address on a card and drop it in a drum. The winner can be notified by mail. Use this technique, and you have the beginnings of a wonderful direct mail list for the next sale.

Good neighbor policies

Be sure that you let the neighbors know about the sale. Be certain that driveways are not blocked, lawns ruined or bad feelings are created by poor crowd control during the days of the sale.

If your library or organization is holding a sale near the business district of town, you might share any printed advertising with those who might benefit from overflow business as a result of the show. You might ask a restaurant, theater or other business to take an ad on the back of a map of the sale or the flyer used for the book sale's publicity to help reduce the cost of printing.

Whenever possible, obtain the advertising, printing and media services as a donation. When you do so, always talk about the books that will be available, learn what books the media representative enjoys, and make an effort to find a gift book for them as the sale is being set up. It's a kindness that will go a long way toward establishing a good relationship for future sales.

Your volunteers are not just for sorting, pricing and setting up the sale. Have them assist in the publicity campaign. They should take the flyers, handbills and posters to their place of employment and have them posted on bulletin boards. No opportunity should be lost to publicize the sale. Your organization must make your book sale the social and cultural event of the month. The library is an ideal focal point for the sale. Readings, additional story hours, and child-oriented events during the sale will be added attractions.

10

Assessing Success

The financial records you kept on expenses and the revenues you have generated will provide you with the tangible evidence of the success of your sale. A record of volunteer time will also be important in estimating the human resources you will need in planning future sales. More difficult to assess will be the intangible costs and benefits. The good will that was generated from the sale will be hard to measure, but one means of assessing it would be to gather the volunteers together to review how the sale went. Collect their comments as a basis for improving the next event. Actually, a party for your volunteers might be a good occasion for this, and be a valuable opportunity to gain their commitment for the next sale.

Consider the impact of your advertising and publicity efforts. Remember that media exposure and coverage after the sale is just as important, if not more so, than pre-event publicity. Trumpet the success of the sale to everyone you can reach. Show tables nearly empty of books. Have photos of smiling customers hauling their treasures out of the sale. Make those who did not attend the sale feel as if they have committed the social error of the year. Tell about all those who helped make the event possible.

Give credit to the radio and television stations who gave air time. Thank all of the merchants and companies who donated time, materials and resources to make the sale possible. Tell the financial figures. Break the sale down into general and special books. Remind the readers how the funds are to be used by the library or organization that sponsored the sale. Thank all those who attended and bought books. Remind the community that it's not too early to begin planning for next year's sale.

Appendix I

A Bibliography on Book Collecting

Ahearn, Allen. *Book Collecting: A Comprehensive Guide*. New York: Putnam, 1989. 320 pp.

> This work provides excellent topical coverage, short and to the point.

Banister, Manly. *Bookbinding As a Handcraft*. New York: Bell, 1975. 160pp.

> A useful introduction to the physical repair of a book. It also explains the terms and techniques used in bookbinding.

Boutell, H. S. *First Editions of To-day and How to Tell Them*. Philadelphia: Lippincott, 1929. 62pp.

> This is a classic work listing the various methods used by publishers through the early twentieth century to indicate first editions.

Bryant, Eric Thomas. *Collecting Gramophone Records*. Westport, CT: Greenwood Press, 1978. 153pp.

> A comprehensive introduction to collecting early recordings. It includes a bibliography of related resources useful in evaluating and pricing these materials.

Buxbaum, Edwin. *Collecting National Geographic Magazines*. Milwaukee: Box Tree Press, 1935. 68pp.

> This is an early history of the magazine with information on highpoints. It may be dated, but it is of great value in assessing the importance of these commonly donated magazines.

Carter, John. *ABC For Book Collectors*. New York: Knopf, 1981. 211pp.

> A dictionary of terms commonly used in book collecting that is both educational and very funny.

Cole, John Young. *Books in Action: The Armed Services Editions*. Washington, DC: Library of Congress, 1984

> Describes the origin and evolution of the Armed Services editions, and how to collect them.

Dunbar, Maurice. *Fundamentals of Book Collecting*. New York: Hermes, 1976. 108pp.

> This is a very concise guide to the basics.

Ethridge, James & Karen Ethridge. *Antiquarian, Specialty, And Used Book Sellers 1993*.Detroit: Omnigraphics, 1993. 523pp.

 This valuable reference tool is a directory which offers subject access to specialties. Entries contain essential information such as hours of service.

Muir, Percy H. (ed.). *Talks on Book Collecting*. London: Cassell, 1952. 105pp.

This work contains an interesting collection of papers delivered by numerous experts.

Peters, Jean. *Collectible Books, Some New Paths*. New York: Bowker, 1979. 294pp.

 Specific topics for study by an authority on book collecting.

Peters, Jean (ed.). *Book Collecting: A Modern Guide*. New York: Bowker, 1977. 288pp.

 How-to guide which will offer many valuable insights into the subject.

Robinson, Ruth E. *Buy Books Where Sell Books Where*. Route 7, Box 162A, Morgantown, WV 26505

 The 1994-1995 guide is 334 pages in length, and it has listings by author, subject and geographic area.

.Siegel, David S. & Susan Siegel. *The Used Book Lover's Guide Series*. Book Hunter Press, P. O. Box 193, Yorktown Heights, NY 10598

 This guide covers different regions of the nation in separate volumes, and each volume is over 300 pages in length. New England, Mid-Atlantic, South Atlantic and Midwest are the areas covered to date. Well organized.

Storm, Colton & Howard Peckham. *Invitation to Book Collecting; Its Pleasures and Practices*. New York: Bowker, 1947. 281pp.

 An attractive manual by two American experts, offering many useful hints.

Tanselle, G. Thomas. *Guide to the Study of United States Imprints*. Cambridge, MA: Harvard, 1971. 2 vols. 1050pp.

 Identifies source material for the study of thousands of American publishers, booksellers, printers, and authors.

Tanselle, G. Thomas. "Book-Jackets, Blurbs, and Bibliographers." In *The Library* (June, 1971) 26:91-134.

 A comprehensive study of the dust jacket.

Targ, William. *Bibliophile in the Nursery, A Bookman's Treasury of Collector's Lore on Old and Rare Children's Books*. Cleveland: World, 1957. 503pp.

 Twenty-three essays by famous bookpeople on children's books.

Winterich, John T. *Collector's Choice*. New York: Greenberg, 1928. 211pp.

 While this is dated, it is a classic which includes more detailed information than the author's more recent edition (*Primer of Book Collecting*).

Winterich, John T. *Primer of Book Collecting*. New York: Bell, 1976. 228pp.

 An overview of the concepts.

Zemple, Edward & Linda Verkler. *A First Edition?* Peoria, IL: Spoon River Press, 1991. Unpaginated.

 Contains the publisher's reports of how editions are identified.

Appendix II

Periodicals

Chernofsky, Jacob. *AB Bookman's Yearbook*. P. O. Box AB Clifton, NJ, 1992

Available as part of a subscription to *AB Bookman's Weekly* or separately. Provides a guide to booksellers with a specialty index, an auction section, and lists of specific books wanted. An important source.

Chernofsky, Jacob. *AB Bookman's Weekly*. P. O. Box AB, Clifton, NJ, 1994

Published 50 weeks of the year, it includes articles, books wanted and books for sale. An essential guide for learning which books are in demand and their valuation.

Smiley, Kathryn. *Firsts: Collecting Modern First Editions*. 575 N. Lucerne Blvd., Los Angeles, CA 90004

A magazine filled with information about fiction, literature and related material. Offers insight to important collectible authors, including first books. Invaluable.

Zemple, Ed. *Bookquote*. 2319-C West Rohmann, Peoria, IL 61604

This is a bi-weekly resource for buyers and sellers of out-of-print, used & rare books. Good introduction.

Appendix III

Price Guides for Book Collectors

Ahearn, Allen & Pat. *Collected Books, The Guide to Values*. New York: Putnam, 1991. 416pp.

Lists prices for books in recent years.

Barnett, Carol. *Botanical and Horticultural Books*. Peoria, IL: Spoon River Press, 1991. 128pp.

Lists the prices of general titles in the field. Provides an excellent introduction.

Books Etc. *Modern Library Price Guide*. San Francisco: Books Etc., 1991. 192pp. (538 Castro St., San Francisco, CA 94114)

Includes all variations on this classic series. This is a sound introduction to a relatively popular edition.

Cole, Michael (ed.). *Annual Register of Book Values*. York, England: The Clique, Annual. 6 vols. (Distributed by Highsmith Press [P.O. Box 800, Ft. Atkinson, WI 53538] to U.S. libraries and institutions.)

A carefully selected compilation of over 30,000 out-of-print books. Each entry contains a full bibliographic citation and a description of the condition or special features of the book with the current market value in U.S. dollars and British sterling. Six convenient subject volumes which are available either individually or as set: *Arts & Architecture, Children's Books, Modern First Editions, Science and Medicine, Literature*, and *Voyages Travel & Exploration*.

Cole, Michael (ed.). *Register of Book Values 92-94*. York, England: The Clique, Annual. CD-ROM (Distributed by Highsmith Press [PO Box 800, Ft. Atkinson, WI 53538] to U.S. libraries and institutions.)

This economical CD-ROM includes eighteen volumes, representing the last three editions of the *Annual Register of Book Values*. Text can be rapidly searched by author, individual words of short text strings. IBM format. Publisher plans to cumulate future ARBV editions in this format

Collins, R. *Mandeville's Used Book Price Guide*. Washington, DC: Price Guide Publishers, 1972 - 1989, 6 vols to date.

Not very selective. A step above "price" guides. Lesser quality books.

Hancer, Kevin & R. Reginald. *Hancer's Price Guide to Paperback Books*. Radnor, PA: Wallace-Homestead, 1990.

Includes information on collecting paper-backs

Jordan, Charles & Donna. *Official Price Guide to Paperbacks & Magazines*. New York: House of Collectibles, 1991.

Contains assessment of magazines as collectibles, with prices.

Leab, K. K. (ed.). *American Book Prices Current*. Washington, CT: Bancroft-Parkman, 1941 –Present.

One volume each year, with index volumes every 5 years. Ninety-six volumes to date. Lists auction prices for books. Does not always reflect condition.

McCarty, Dennis. *Books About Books*. Clarendon Hills, IL: Willow Press, 1985. 78pp.

A small price guide that describes the condition of some collectible books.

McCarty, Dennis. *Western Americana*. Clarendon Hills, IL: Willow Press, 1987. 159pp.

A substantial reference book showing a range of values. It does not include a description of the condition.

McGrath, Daniel. *Bookman's Price Index*. Detroit: Gale, 1966 - present.

One volume each year, 42 to date. Contains the prices for books compiled from booksellers' catalogs. Does not tell overall condition, or if the book was sold for the price listed.

Sheets, K. A. *American Fishing Books 1743 - 1993: A Guide to Values*. Ann Arbor, MI: Anglers & Scholars, 1993, 111pp. (K. A. Sheets Rare Books, P. O. Box 7024, Ann Arbor, MI 48107)

Lists those books published in America on fishing. Contains prices.

Warren, Jon R. *The Official Price Guide, Paperbacks*. New York: House of Collectibles, 1991. 934pp.

Includes prices for series books.

Warth, Thomas. *Car Book Value Guide*. Marine, MN: Tew Press, 1991. 173pp. (Tew Press, Lumberyard Shops, Marine, MN 55047)

Lists 5,000 titles by author, subject, value and title. A bibliographical tool as well.

Zemple, Ed and Linda Verkler. *Book Prices: Used and Rare*. Peoria, IL: Spoon River Press, Annual. (Spoon River Press, 2319-C West Rohmann, Peoria, IL 61604)

Started in 1993, this huge reference includes a broad range of titles. Alphabetical by author. Includes condition.

Appendix IV

Volunteers

Bortin, Virginia. *Publicity for Volunteers: A Handbook.* New York: Walker, 1981. 159pp.

A concise guide on the development of publicity.

Ducas, Dorothy. *Working With Volunteers.* New York: Foundation for Public Relations, 1977. 16pp.

A very brief but useful pamphlet on basic steps in the effective use of volunteers within an organization.

Fisher, James. *Leadership and Management of Volunteer Programs: A Guide for Volunteer Administrators.* San Francisco: Jossey-Bass, 1993. 208pp.

Recent publication of value to volunteer coordinators, and to the organizations that have initiated volunteer support programs.

Karp, Rashelle S. *Volunteers in the Small Library.* Chicago: American Library Association, 1992. 16pp.

One of the Small Libraries Publication series that explains how to integrate volunteers into the overall services program.

McCurley, Stephen and Rick Lynch. *Essential Volunteer Management.* Downers Grove, IL: VM Systems, 1989. 136pp.

Stresses the management role in maintaining effective volunteer activities.

Weiner, Harold N. *Making the Most of Special Events.* New York: National Communication Council, 1977. 20pp.

Describes the role of volunteers in the planning and implementation of special events.

Appendix V

A Guide to Simple Book Repairs

Repair of donated books is time consuming and can only be attempted on those that hold the promise of better value. Once you become proficient at these methods, a repair person will be able to perform six or more repairs in an hour for separated or broken hinges and many more for loose hinges.

Inner hinge repair

When better books are received, condition is imperative in receiving a better price. One of the most common condition defects is loose inner hinges. The binding or cloth covered boards begin to separate from the book itself, and the book moves around freely within the binding. If the hinges are not cracked or broken, repair is very easy.

Obtain an long, thin metal rod, of coat hanger diameter or even thinner if possible. Lay the book flat, and coat the metal rod with a good liquid paste such as Highsmith Book-Saver® or wheat paste. Run the paste coated rod under the endpaper between the spine and the hinge and apply a coating of paste.

Cover the endpapers with a sheet of wax paper, and close the cover. Next, insert a piece of metal the diameter of a clothes hanger on the outer joint and place a weight on the book to retain the original shape of the gutter along the spine and front cover. Repeat the procedure for the rear cover if it is loose. Allow the book to dry overnight.

Tightening the book in its binding will provide a solid repair that will prevent any apologies about a book's condition and allow you to ask a more rewarding price.

Broken hinge repair

If a book with increased value is received with the inner hinges broken, they can still be repaired. Obtain a 1-1/2 inch wide piece of Japanese Mulberry paper cut 1/2 inch longer than the inside measure of the book. Bring the separated cover and book together and hold the spine of the cover in place with a weight. Paste any remnants of the endpapers back into place. Then apply paste to the mulberry paper, and place it over the separated hinge. Be sure that the repair strip is even across the broken hinge, before smoothing with a bone folder.

Place a piece of wax paper on your work surface, turn the book over and repeat the procedure for the rear hinge. Then with the boards open toward the spine, stand the book carefully to dry.

In a few hours the hinges will be dry. The book will be reset in its binding, and value will be recovered. Be sure to notify any prospective customer that the book has been repaired.

Wheat paste

Many library suppliers sell good quality paste designed specifically for books, such as Highsmith Book-Saver®. However, if you wish to prepare your own, one of the easiest materials for book repair is wheat paste. Add one cup of cold water to a small sauce pan. Measure two heaping tablespoons of flour. Begin heating the water and slowly add the flour while stirring rapidly. Bring the water to a boil while continuing to stir. Boil for three minutes and set aside to cool. Place the completed wheat paste in a jar, cap tightly and store in the refrigerator. The paste will last about two weeks.

Japanese mulberry paper

This light, but surprisingly strong paper can be purchased in large sheets at most art supply stores. It is an extremely valuable resource for repairing damage in books which have good resale potential. Incidentally, always remember never to use general purpose transparent tape in mending torn pages, since it will eventually cause the paper to deteriorate. Many suppliers do sell transparent tape that is safe.

Mending and binding supplies

A source for book repair supplies is:

Highsmith, Inc.
P.O. Box 800
Ft. Atkinson, WI 53538-0800

Call toll free 1-800-558-2110 for a free catalog or to order supplies. Highsmith also sells *Care & Repair: Book Saving Techniques: A Guide to Basic Care & Repair* (Ft. Atkinson, WI: Highsmith, 1990. 24pp.). The illustrations and information that follow are from this guide.

or
University Products, Inc.
517 Main St.
PO Box 101
Holyoak, MA 01040-0101

Another special source for binding supplies is:

The Bookbinder's Warehouse Inc.
31 Division Street
Keyport, NJ 07735

Call (908) 264-0306 and ask for their catalog.

MONEY-SAVING REPAIRS

REPLACING A LOOSE PAGE WITH BOOK-SAVER®

Materials Needed:
Book-Saver®	Rubber Bands
Book Weight	Wax Paper
Mending Stick	Scissors

 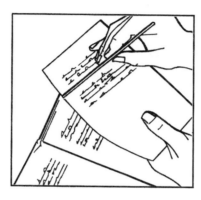 

1. Make sure the inside edge of the loose page is smooth. If not, trim carefully using scissors, cutting only what is necessary to create a straight edge.

2. Taking care not to damage the spine, spread the book open as far as possible. Place wax paper on either side of where the loose page is to be inserted. Apply a thin coating of Book-Saver by gently rolling the mending stick along the inside edge of the loose page.

3. Insert the glued edge into the open book, making sure the page is aligned at the top, side and bottom with the rest of the bound pages.

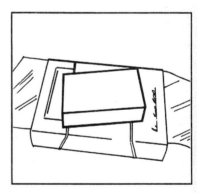

4. Close the book and wrap rubber bands around it. Place the book under weights until the Book-Saver is thoroughly dry.

Note: If more than one page is loose, allow ample drying time between each page. Do not attempt to glue all pages back in at once. If multiple pages are loose, consider having the book professionally rebound.

Source: *Care & Repair: Book Saving Techniques: A Guide to Basic Care & Repair* (Ft. Atkinson, WI: Highsmith, 1990) p. 8.

MONEY-SAVING REPAIRS

REPAIRING LOOSE HINGES:

Materials Needed:
Book-Saver®   Book Weight
Bone Folder   Rubber Band
Mending Stick   Knitting Needles or
Paper Hinge Tape   Dowels

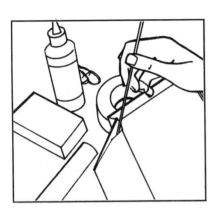

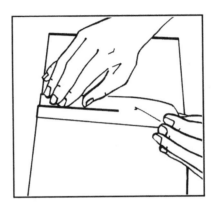

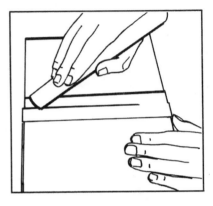

1. Lightly coat a mending stick with Book-Saver and insert carefully between the endsheet and the cover. **Caution:** Never place adhesive down the spine of the book.

2. Cut a strip of paper hinge tape to the length of your book. Apply to the endsheet and fly leaf.

3. Use your plastic bone folder to smooth the tape and gently crease the hinge.

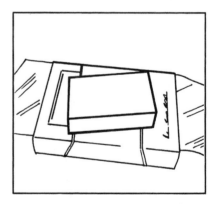

4. Place dowels or knitting needles in joints on front and back cover and rubber band securely. Place book under weight to allow Book-Saver to dry.

Source: *Care & Repair: Book Saving Techniques: A Guide to Basic Care & Repair* (Ft. Atkinson, WI: Highsmith, 1990) p. 12.

Appendix VI

Glossary

Booksellers have a unique set of terms used to describe features of a book's condition, as well as the construction of the book, physical attributes and special jargon. This list will make the rules, conventions and specialized useage easier to decipher.

For an exhaustive study of these terms, see John Carter's riotous *ABC for Book Collectors*.

Glossary terms

as issued - Describes the physical attributes of a book, such as "without the dust jacket," as issued.

association copy - Having a connection with the author, an important acquaintance of the author or other historically significant individual.

bibliomania - A condition afflicting book collectors.

bindings - Most books are inserted in cases of either cloth or paper today and not really bound. Cloth describes a set of boards covered by a cloth material, the same as hardcover. Paperbacks have a heavy paper cover, while leather bindings are usually the genuine item.

book club - An edition of a book often published in a different cloth, in a smaller format, and with different paper. All or some of the above may be true. Book club editions will often state their identity on the dust jacket of the book, or there will be a circular, triangular or square stamped indentation on the back cover in the cloth close to the spine.

book plate - A device afixed to the front endpaper pasted to the inside book cover noting the ownership of the book. The bookplate is often very attractive and might even be collected in its own right.

condition - This is important when describing a book by mail or over the phone to a potential customer. The following terms are those used by most members of the bookselling and collecting community. By convention, the usual method of description is to start with the description of the exterior, describe the dust jacket if issued, then move to the contents of the book. Whenever possible, avoid the statement, "very good for its age." Such words might disturb collectors or dealers. A book published in 1775 and well maintained may be just as good as one delivered in a used condition in 1994.

as new - Describes the book's condition as it would have been when first published.

fine - Similar to above, but with a general appearance of not being as sharp as new.

very good - A used book that shows some sign of use and minor wear or rubbing to the cloth or dust jacket. Any tears, writing or defects must be noted.

good - The average condition of a used book, describing both the dust jacket and the binding. Note any problems such as underlining or marginal notes. The contents are tight in the binding.

fair - The text of the book is complete, but is worn, loose, perhaps with endpapers missing, torn pages and other defects.

poor - So worn as to serve only as a reference or reading copy. Plates or other illustrations may be missing, but the text is extant. Wear would include stains, marks, writing, defective hinges either inside or out, pages falling out, etc.

else fine - A laughable phrase invented by amateurs in the business in an attempt to make glaring defects of condition more palatable. Examples would be, "All color plates removed, Crayon notations in an infantile hand," else fine.

copyright - The statement of ownership and often associated with the date the book first appeared in print. See First Edition.

disbound - Removed from a binding, or serial works cut up.

dust jacket - The paper wrapper around most modern books. It is a marketing tool to get your attention. Designed to protect the underlying binding, they first began appearing just before the turn of the twentieth century. They are important in keeping the book "as issued."

edition - An edition of a work represents all books printed from one setting of the type or format without significant changes. Any substantial change to the contents constitutes a new edition.

endpapers - The blank pages at the beginning or end of the book. There are two pairs. The first pair is referred to as the front, where one is pasted down on the inside front board or cover and the other is the free endpaper, The rear endpapers are a similar pair of free and pasted pages.

ex-library - Any book that has been part of a lending library. There will often be spine labels or numbers, a card pocket on one of the endpapers, and ownership stamps placed on the inner pages of the book. Ex-Library books may not be in bad condition. However, they contain excessive marks of previous ownership.

first edition - As a common denominator, the first appearance of a book in print.

fly leaf - Often confused with endpapers, the fly leaves are placed as blank sheets by the publisher after the endpapers to make the signatures of a book even.

format - Describes the size of a book. Measurements are approximate.

folio - A large book made of printing sheets folded in half: 20" x 14"

quarto - Pages folded in fourths: (4to) 11" x 9"

octavo - Pages folded in eighths: (8vo) 9" x 6"

duodecimo - Pages folded in twelveths: (12mo) 5" x 3"

foxing - Paper that is irregularly discolored or browned.

frontispiece - Picture or illustration that faces the title page.

gatherings - Folded pages of a book arranged in signatures and derived from the format of the book.

gilt edges - Refers to gold applied to one or more edges of a book: t.e.g. is the top edge gilt, a.e.g. all edges gilt, and f.e.g. foredge gilt.

half-title - The page before the frontispiece and title page which has the title of the book and other information.

hinges - Inside point where the binding joins the book. Covered by the endpapers.

impression - Number of books printed at one time of any edition, such as the fourth impression of the first edition.

inscribed - A note from the author to someone.

joints - The outer juncture of the spine with the covers.

limited edition - Any publication which has a set number of copies, such as #413 of 500 copies.

points - Words or differences in books from one edition or impression to another.

presentation copy - A gift from the author to the recipient.

provenance - The trail of who owned a particular title.

reading copy - A book that is not suitable as a collectible, but acceptable if you can't wait to own a book you've sought for years.

sophisticated - A book that has been made too new.

uncut - The edges of the book have not been trimmed; they are uneven.

unopened - The edges of the book with the foldings intact. You cannot open the pages to look inside.

working copy - A book that is in such poor condition that you are embarrassed to own it, except that you need it to complete some research.

Appendix VII

A Book Sale Checklist

Lead time for planning and implementing your book sale will depend on the size of the event and the resources available to you and your organization. However, you will want to ensure that there will be enough time to accomplish the following basis steps. Use this simple checklist to establish a timetable.

1. Plan the date for the event, preferably one that has as few conflicts as possible. Be mindful of holidays and other special events in the area. Check with the local and area chambers of commerce.

2. Determine the type of materials to be sold, and plan a campaign to solicit donations. Set a goal for the number of books and other materials you hope to collect, and an estimated profit after expenses.

3. Secure a place (or places) for storage, sorting and holding the sale, and collect containers for proper storage.

4. Assemble a volunteer staff, and assign work responsibilities. Arrange for any needed training and resources for pricing books.

5. Categorize, sort, and price the donations while training the volunteer staff for minor mending and book evaluation.

6. Develop a floor plan for the sale, with sufficient room for display and storage of the books.

7. Determine the number of tables, chairs and other supplies that will be needed for the sale, and arrange for their delivery.

8. Have sufficient change and cash boxes. Make certain to obtain a sales permit if this is required in your state or locality, and make arrangements for the collection and payment of sales taxes if required.

9. Schedule work hours, break times and plan for refreshments for the volunteers.

10. Prepare category signs for all tables of books.

11. Generate publicity, in print, radio and posters around town. Location, date, times, special deals on prices should be stressed.

12. Acknowledge the donation of in-kind, goods, services and other assistance whenever possible. Thank your volunteers.

Index